A Flickering Flame

Creative Strategies For Crises Intervention

CURTIS L. WHITNEY

WestBow Press books may be ordered through booksellers or by contacting:

WestBow Press
A Division of Thomas Nelson & Zondervan
1663 Liberty Drive
Bloomington, IN 47403
www.westbowpress.com
1 (866) 928-1240

ISBN: 978-1-9736-6439-0 (sc)
ISBN: 978-1-9736-6440-6 (hc)
ISBN: 978-1-9736-6438-3 (e)

Library of Congress Control Number: 2019906642

Print information available on the last page.

WestBow Press rev. date: 6/11/2019

Contents

Foreword

I accepted my call to the ministry at a very young age and began my pastoral career at an equally young age. During that time, the excitement of ministry was high, and the desire to succeed (whatever that means as it relates to ministry) was great. I had also grown up in church and around seasoned pastors and was privy to a lot of conversations. However, I was blessed to have a pastor who taught me how to be a pastor (as much as that may be possible). He taught me how to love people, care for people, and care for myself.

In 1 Corinthians 4:14, 15, the apostle Paul writes, "I write not these things to shame you, but as my beloved sons I warn you. For though ye have ten thousand instructors in Christ yet have ye not many fathers: for in Christ Jesus I have begotten you through the gospel." Some pastors may not have had the active presence of a "father-in-ministry," which can make pastoral ministry quite challenging. Many people will give you plenty of advice but not be present to help you navigate the maze of ministry. Therefore, you will be left to trial and error.

The work presented by Dr. Curtis Whitney is invaluable because it comes from the heart and life of a seasoned pastor who becomes vulnerable to the reader for the purpose of instruction. He is very clear, very practical, and quite insightful as he shares his decades of experience in dealing with the intricacies of ministry (i.e., how to set up a congregational care system, how to address congregational vulnerabilities, etc.). He is not so theoretical in this work that he omits the practical, but his practicality is biblically based. Both the practical and the theoretical are necessary to do the work of ministry.

I have spent thirty-five years in ministry, with thirty of those years in the pastorate. I am in the beginning stages of considering the final years of actively pastoring. I have watched many pastors overstay their season and have seen very vibrant and influential congregations decline significantly. Although the reasons have varied—from identity to no successors—the need to plan for the inevitable is critical. Preparing for the future is, too, a part of taking care of ourselves and the people we serve. Dr. Curtis Whitney, whom I respect highly for his pastoral prowess and ministerial integrity, provides for us the framework for discerning the seasons of ministry

Based on his decades of pastoral service and dedication, Dr. Whitney writes very transparently and provides for us both research and empirical data to help us manage that flickering flame.

Dr. Whitney very clearly teaches us that caring for our congregations through the implementation of productive programs, understanding that self-care is not some inflated sense of self-importance, and discerning the times is paramount. It is a realistic view of a healthy pastor serving a healthy congregation while being faithful God.

Dr. Whitney's work is like an automobile maintenance manual. It reminds us that we must stop for fuel, check the oil levels, be sure the tires are properly inflated, and get regular tune-ups. He helps us to recognize those weird noises and address those issues. Listen to a voice of one who has been where many of us have yet to go; listen to the voice of experience. You owe it to the people you serve; you owe it to your family. You owe it to yourself. You owe it to God.

Bishop W. James Thomas II, DMin
Senior Pastor, Calvary Baptist
Church Dover, Delaware

Acknowledgments

A Flickering Flame was conceived early in my life. It is a work prompted and supported by countless individuals whose shoulders I have stood upon. I owe a huge debt of gratitude to many who were stakeholders in my growth and development.

Thanks to my praying parents who have been called home from labor to reward, Deacon Robert and Deaconess Juanita Whitney, for their example of how Christians should live during times of great oppression. They sacrificed much so that their eleven children had food on the table, clothes on our backs, and a roof over our heads. Ruth and I are grateful for our precious children, Heide and Keith, whose memory we honor as they have taken their place in the celestial choir. I can't forget to say thanks to our only surviving child, Monique, in sharing insight into the writing of this book and giving birth to our precious granddaughter, Kennedy Luna. Thanks to Matthew and Vilma Wilson (our deceased daughter Heide's son and daughter in-law) for their encouragement and giving birth to our great-granddaughter Vanessa. Thanks to Janika Wilson, our granddaughter for always keeping our spirits high with her unique source of support.

I thank God for the Reverend Curtis Proctor, the first pastor of Ebenezer Baptist Church in Ivor, Virginia, who baptized me at the age of ten.

My appreciation goes to the Reverend R. P. Means, pastor of the Abyssinian Baptist Church in Newark, New Jersey, who nurtured and encouraged me to get on the right path. This was during wild and restless adolescent years, when I was without parental guidance.

Many thanks to Reverend L. E. Terrell of the Union Baptist Church in Harlem, New York, who gave me an opportunity to become a deacon and later a minister of the Gospel of Jesus Christ.

Special gratitude to the late Reverend Dr. Ollie B. Wells for his untiring efforts in equipping and elevating me to minister of education at the Union Baptist Church in Harlem, New York.

I am truly grateful to God that he allowed me the opportunity to sit at the feet of some of the greatest biblical scholars that could be found anywhere: (1) the late Dr. James Washington, (2) the late Dr. James Cone, and (3) living legends Drs. James A. Forbes and Cornell West. Thanks for their wisdom and scholarly encouragement.

I enthusiastically applaud these senior sages, who fed us with nutritious food from the master's table. Many have crossed over the Jordan, but the melody of their influence still lingers: Reverend Dr. Gardner C. Taylor, the prince of preachers; Reverend Dr. Sandy F. Ray; Dr. Robert Laws; Reverend Dr. Samuel Austin; Reverend Dr. Spurgeon E. Crayton; Reverend Dr. H. Devore Chapman; Reverend Dr. W. J. Hall, and the Reverend W. Lymon Lowe. I'm grateful for those who are still holding up the banner: Reverend William Bunton and Dr. Washington Lundy.

Thanks to the young pastors I call my sons and daughters, who have been a great inspiration and support: Reverend Larry W. Camp, Reverend Carl A. Leach, Reverend Willard Finerson, Reverend Dr. Gary Simpson, Reverend Timothy Taylor, Reverend Randy Maxwell, Reverend David Cousin, Reverend Valerie Cousin, Reverend Kim Neal, and Reverend Dr. Carl Washington. Reverend Jason Rideout (adopted son in Little Rock, Arkansas), I appreciate the book cover design. Special thanks to Reverend Tim and Kim Hunter.

Thanks to Bishop Phillip E. Elliott, pastor of Antioch Baptist Church in Hempstead, New York

Special thanks to my church of thirty-two years, the Mount Sinai Baptist Church in Brooklyn, New York, for allowing me to share my gifts and provide leadership in building the community and transforming lives.

A very special thanks my wife, Ruth, of fifty-seven years, who provided invaluable service in the proofreading and organization of the manuscript. Kudos to Monique, my only remaining child, who gave insightful suggestions for marketing this book. Praise God for my seven living siblings and four deceased, who allowed me to play church and preach to them when we had nothing else to do.

To my pastor, Bishop W. James Thomas II, for his anointed and powerful messages each week. To his lovely wife, Elder Antonia Thomas, and the Calvary Baptist Church in Dover, Delaware, thank you for embracing my family with open arms and agape love.

Preface
Ministry Matters

Across the vast expanse of fifty years, crisscrossing local, state, national, and international borders, I have been the recipient of inspiration and information by attending numerous seminars, workshops, and conventions. At many I have been given the honor and opportunity to share my gift in pastoral care and counseling for the body of Christ.

What concerns me most is the fact little attention has been focused on the church's response to the care of souls in a culture dominated by crises such as public shootings at schools and places of worship. During my fifty years in ministry, not only have I observed the proliferation of crises on a personal front but on a wider one as well. In the height of my pastoral ministry, I experienced the death of both parents, several siblings, and two children—a daughter and only son.

A Flickering Flame explores how effective intervention can be initiated and implemented in congregational crises, resulting in a healthy body of baptized believers. The title describes how a people so empowered can rise to the occasion and while the flame may flicker, assured assistance will be provided to keep it aglow. Growing up in a small and impoverished sharecropping community in Southampton County, Virginia (Nat Turner country), failed to prepare me to make a significant difference in the lives of the faith community. I often raised the question where would this road lead? What could I do to change my present condition? Also, how would I know when I had reached the road to which God was directing me? There were a lot of questions and few answers.

Introduction
A Flickering Flame

I have always been fascinated by a flickering flame. As a young boy growing up in a family of eleven siblings, we were assigned special tasks. My parents implemented this plan to ensure that everything ran smoothly. The task given to me was providing enough wood for the fireplace. I spent a considerable amount of time watching the flame flicker. If the flame continued to flicker, it was signaling that immediate intervention was needed to keep the fire burning.

Once I accepted the call to ministry and began interacting with people from all walks of life, it became clear that we are all subject to life crises from birth to death.

At an early age, I felt an insatiable passion that propelled me to make life better for persons struggling to resolve the difficult crises they faced from day to day. In helping care for these persons, they would be able to endure with dignity and hope during their peril and plight. It's a reality that before we can get through one crisis, we are headed into another. Crises are the order of the day. Many times, these events or accidents come our way and are often unexpected. The one we all remember is that infamous terrorist attack of 9/11, when thousands of persons lost their lives. It is true that life is punctuated by circumstances that would cause our flames to flicker. The flame that has been burning brightly is now flickering and is in danger of being blown out. I have listened empathetically to persons who have lamented how they have managed to build a future over decades only to see it destroyed in minutes. For some, it might have been a hurricane or tornado, and for others it has been an earthquake, tsunami, fire, or flood. We have witnessed public shootings in schools, houses of worship, and other environments.

As the journey begins, chapter 1 describes a sketch of my personal history and how it has impacted my pastoral identity. The history will be highlighted by German American developmental psychologist Erik Erikson's eight stages of human growth and development. Each stage, as you will see, contains the opportunity for the occurrence of crisis.

Chapter 2 discusses the relevance of historical perspective of the ministry context and the necessity for such an endeavor. Chapter 3 identifies the team selection and their professional preparation. Chapter 4 examines the biblical model for a caring community and a description of that city that's set on a hill (Matthew 5:14 KJV). Despite the many crises that have affected members of the African American congregation and caused its flame to flicker, it continues to be that city on a hill. Its light cannot be hidden.

Chapter 5 explores theological foundations, including some themes of black theology and practical aspects of the program. Chapter 6 addresses the social science foundation. Chapter 7 lists the outline of the training resources for caregivers.

Chapter 8 deals with a specific matter that should be top priority for the spiritual leader—namely, navigating pastoral pitfalls. Chapter 9 presents insights and wisdom as one is cruising into the twilight of retirement and deciding when it's time to leave. And then comes the conclusion.

Equally important are efforts to create a significant program of professional training that pertains not only to the clergy but laity as well. It is my heartfelt conviction that the principles of faith and practice are desperately needed for the people of God who have faced oppression, whether political, economic, physical, or spiritual needs and care. The body of Christ therefore must be engaged in responding to the liberating experience of a pastoral care program that addresses the deficit of literature that seems to be forgotten and lost in trivial pursuits.

We are all traveling on the highway of life and unfortunately will encounter some mishaps, such as a flat tire that might necessitate roadside assistance. Being engaged in ministry for more than five decades, I have met many wearied travelers who have experienced menacing moments when it seemed that they were on the brink of some sort of breakdown. It is at this point the light begins to flicker.

This book discusses the need I found to actively involve laypersons in a program of short-term crisis care at the Mt. Sinai Baptist Church in Brooklyn, New York. The rationale for writing such a book is predicated on the need for a more productive ministry in helping members through personal crises. This necessitated the selection and training of fifteen laypersons who would be equipped to assist in providing ongoing pastoral care.

In response to the requirement for the doctor of ministry degree, I was confident that this program would accrue unlimited value. This holds true not only for the Mt. Sinai Baptist Church in Brooklyn but every church, especially the black church, which must bear the burden and glory of offering to a suffering people light and hope that transcends the human predicament. To this end, this title has been conceived.

While a student at Drew University, I completed a reading assignment for a book written by James C. Fenhagen, which served as a powerful influence in shaping my choice of deciding what directions to take for my doctor of ministry dissertation. It inspired me to revisit my life journey and seriously consider a ministry of liberation and healing within the body of Christ.

It stated:

> The Christian journey is not a journey from somewhere to nowhere. It is a journey from self-awareness to an ever-deepening communion with God, expressed in an ever- deepening compassion for the world. It is a journey in which our own unfolding story becomes more and more in tune with the biblical story of redemption. It is essential, therefore, that our journey be grounded in the tradition from which it draws life![1]

All of God's people have a story that is incomplete and unfolding from day to day. Woven into the saga of our stories is the fabric that makes us who we are and will either cause us to stumble or rise to new heights. There will be times when our lights might flicker, but someone will show up to keep them aglow. One thing that I've learned in my years of ministry is that there is a world of hurting people in the congregation and the marketplace ready to fall off the slippery slopes of destruction. They are desperately searching for help that will offer them hope and a reason to go on. This condition is best described by the metaphor of a flickering flame. There are countless persons journeying on the highway of life, stranded in the darkness while trying to figure out how to get out of this existential predicament. Imagine a lonely traveler on a deserted highway encountering the unfortunate occurrence of a flat tire. He pulls over to the side of road. He realizes the only source of light is one match. The wind is blowing, and he is desperately waving for help from some stranger to stop and give assistance in protecting the flame long enough to remove the flat tire and replace the spare.

On this journey of life, we will need help as we encounter uncertain turns or accidents. The good news is that there is a special group of roadside assistants known as clergy. I am proud to have been a part of this special group for the past fifty years.

The thesis of this book is that from the cradle to the grave, we face eight critical stages of psychosocial development. The idea is that if needs are adequately met in each stage, then one is prepared to move to the next stage without bringing along unresolved issues. This may cause our lives to flicker. As roadside assistants, we have the responsibility of providing help to the wearied travelers on the highway of life.

As the words of Ira Wilson's hymn reminded me, I caught the vision and my calling became clear.

Out in the highways and byways of life,
Many are weary and sad;
Carry the sunshine where darkness is rife,
Making the sorrowing glad.

Make me a blessing, make me a blessing,
Out of my life may Jesus shine;
Make me a blessing, O Savior, I pray,
Make me a blessing to someone today.[2]

Jesus recognized that need in people and quickly responded appropriately. Whether He was teaching among crowds, passing along the seashore, or walking the dusty roads of Jerusalem, He was responsive to human hurting. He healed people's deepest pain and provided comfort for their most profound needs.

As I reflect over my many years of ministry, I am determined to leave some trace of God's grace that has impacted me. I hope that in sharing my story, someone might be helped.

It is my hope that the value and need for this writing will give assistance to those coming after me when their lights flicker.

There is a poem written by an unknown author that can best explain my intention:

The Bridge Builder

An old man came down the road of life,
to a chasm wide and deep
He spent much time on the downward climb,
Then scaled the walls so steep
And when he got to the other side,
he set to build a bridge
He'd build it safe and strong,
so it would span from ridge to ridge
He labored on to build it strong
with sturdy beams and piers
To span life's deep dark valley
and its swirling river of tears
And when he finished°... standing near°... [3]

I believe by sharing my personal history is a good way to inspire others by example. It is also to show how God can take the crises in one's life and transform them into something good.

Seldom does one begin a journey without some sense of anxiety or uncertainty. Not everyone who goes down the same path as we do will be confronted by the same experiences, but they will probably be similar. It is my intention to share some of my experiences from my personal journey that led me to answer the call that God placed on my life.

It is my desire that readers will learn and be empowered by my personal struggles and wisdom. I hope it will help you discern the call of God in your life, and you will say yes to His call. In the process of saying yes, at times the flame may flicker as if it will go out, but there will be those who come along for you as they did for me, whose presence reassured me and helped me keep the flame aglow.

There has been pain, suffering, and despair along the way, but God has used this as the raw material to authenticate my person and show that this is all part of the landscape one encounters on the journey to the Promised Land. This journey at times has been like driving at night and suddenly encountering fog. Joy Laughridge puts it this way:

> Even amid tragedy and suffering, especially in either our own or others, this is our opportunity to express and share our faith that the way things are now isn't the way that they will always be. It is an opportunity to proclaim that the forces which oppose God now will not be permitted to oppose God forever. It is our chance to invite and call others to trust and believe in Jesus with us and to join us in following him.[4]

At points you cannot see, but then the fog lifts and you are able to make progress again. Along the way, I have come to cross roads that have been difficult to navigate, but there was that drive to go forward. As God continued to guide and direct, He pointed out the desired route and turned my private pain into public praise. The following chapter describes my personal history and pastoral identity.

Chapter 1
Personal History and Pastoral Identity

Every journey has a starting point. This is the point where our life stories begin.

Events and experiences during the early stages of human growth and development are not easily remembered. Nevertheless, it is during this time that we are given opportunities to embrace that will either lift us up or pull us down. Each stage has a positive side as well as a negative side.

What I accomplished in life, my worldview, is based on how I responded to the eight life cycles as given by Erik Ericson.

Trust vs. Mistrust of Infancy (age 0-1½)

Growing up in a small community, I don't remember any significant events during the early stages of my life. This was because there was little or no social outlet, only church and school. However, I felt that I was special in the eyes of my parents. I felt especially close to Mom. She provided consistent and reliable care, thus giving me a sense of warmth and security. Being given this quality of care, I was able to develop a feeling of trust in those around me. Consequently, I experienced a great love for people, and there was the mutual joy of building relationships.

Autonomy vs. Shame and Doubt (age 1 1/2-3).

During this time, I began asserting my independence, deciding which toy to play with or making choices about what I would eat or wear. Since there was little or no opportunity for independence, I accepted what was available. I made my own toys because playmates were few and far between.

Dad found the time to read me many biblical stories, which I found fascinating.

Initiative vs. Guilt (age 3-5)

As I embraced this period of development, I began interacting with other children at church school. There weren't that many games to play or children in the neighborhood to play with. These were days when video games were unheard of. Very few resources were available from which to choose. This was a period when racial segregation was part of my very existence. Dealing with the mean system of segregation was a devastating blow to my God-given initiative. I began to get a sense of my purpose in life. However, it was a struggle. One of the most significant experiences of this stage was sitting on Dad's lap and listening to him read many of the biblical stories of ancient Israel.

Industry vs. Inferiority (age 5-12)

School age was a time when teachers began to play an important role in my life. I was taught specific skills that increased self-esteem. During this period, I began spending a great amount of time reading and writing. In fact, I began writing with my left hand but decided to change to my right hand instead.

Early school years were very much like home. I was signaled out as special and consequently received the nickname "Teacher's Pet." The teacher always assigned me the task of monitoring the class while she was out of the classroom. However, this special status had its drawbacks. It was not long before my peers resented my being given this special status. The light began to flicker as I began to struggle with acceptance due to bullying.

Adolescence Ego Identity vs. Role Confusion (age 12-18)

This stage was very challenging to me as I began looking toward the future in terms of vocation and relationships. I spent considerable time reading, especially biblical stories that somehow motivated me to fully explore God's creation.

I felt convinced that it was time to move to a different environment since my immediate environment did not offer any prospects of helping me get to where I wanted to go. With a limited background in life, like Abraham, I heard the voice of God say, "Get thee from among your kindred and acquaintances and go to a land that I will show you." This two-letter word *go* has done wonders in shaping and guiding my ministry.

Intimacy vs. Isolation (age18-40)

I felt I was at the crossroads of my life. The first seventeen years of my life were spent on a farm in Virginia where I lived with my parents and ten siblings. During my preadolescent years, I realized this small community did not provide the opportunity to assist me to where I wanted to go. Dad worked extremely hard on the farm just to provide the family with food, clothing, shelter, and education. Mom did her best to take care of us while Dad worked.

Once out of the home and school setting, I discovered that life was different.

Upon graduation from high school with honors, I began studies at Virginia State University with a major in business administration. Even though tuition was inexpensive, Dad could not provide even the least amount of assistance. Consequently, I worked on campus while studying to get a two-year degree. I moved to Richmond, Virginia, and then to Newark, New Jersey, where I enlisted in the US Army. The army was a great help in getting me started on a path that eventually led me to developing my faith journey.

This journey took me to Bamberg, Germany. While stationed in Germany, I was exposed to a different culture and found it very exciting. Having received an honorable discharge, I returned to Newark, New Jersey. While contemplating my next step in life, I could still hear that small voice saying, "Go." This led me to a church in New York City. Going to this church was an opportunity to reunite with an army buddy I met while in Bamberg, Germany. This was the beginning of my conversion experience, and it served as a benchmark of God shaping my personal identity. I was willing to take the initiative to go where I believed God was leading me. The church was not impressive to say the least. It was a small storefront with a Pentecostal atmosphere. I did not know what to expect. I was slightly uncomfortable because I had not been exposed to a lot of hand clapping, shouting, and saying amen. It was in this service that led to my conversion experience. From that moment on, I had a zeal to share this experience with others.

In the excitement of this newly found religious experience, my sister introduced me to a charming young lady (my wife, Ruth). It was love at first sight, for we both had been praying for our soul mate. We were engaged on our first date. After marriage, it was evident that God had special work for us to do. Shortly thereafter, that word *go* surfaced once again. I was led to Union Baptist Churches in Harlem, New York. I was assigned to teach Sunday school, became a member of the diaconate, and was later licensed and ordained to the gospel ministry. For the first time in my life, church involvement took on new meaning. I now felt that I was on the road I had been searching for. Union was the church that provided a passport to Christian ministry. I began to pray and study the Word. I felt the call to ministry. The Lord laid upon my heart to "study to show yourself approved a workman that needeth not to be ashamed rightly dividing the word of truth"(2 Tim 2:15KJV).

At this juncture, I felt inadequate to answer the call. I applied for GI Bill financial assistance and enrolled at Queens College. At the end of my first year there, I became interim minister of the Mount Ararat Baptist Church in Rutherford, New Jersey. I assumed the duties of pastor during the transition of calling a full-time pastor. The Rutherford congregation was an interracial middle-class community that provided an excellent context for one learning what ministry is all about. The people were very accepting and open to change.

While attending Queens College in the evening, I held a full-time supervisory position at American Express. This position provided training in various skills for managing interpersonal relationships. I received a bachelor of arts degree in psychology from Queens College and a master of divinity from the Union Theological Seminary in New York City in 1986. I then served as interim minister of the Soundview Presbyterian Church in Bronx, New York. This experience was most fruitful for it exposed me to a different denomination. At the end of this assignment, I returned to my former church, where I was appointed to serve as minister of Christian education.

Meanwhile, a young congregation in Westbury, Long Island—St. Johns Baptist Church—called me to serve as its second pastor. I accepted the call. After providing five years of quality leadership to this congregation, I realized I could no longer lead it to greener pastures.

After twenty-one years of service at American Express, God propelled me into full-time ministry to exercise my gift of administration in many of the local, state, and national churches and associations. It was during this period that my ministry really grew.

Generativity vs. Stagnation Adulthood (age 40-65)

I was called to the Mount Sinai Baptist Church in Brooklyn, New York, in 1984 as the fourth senior pastor after serving over a year as assistant to the pastor. I answered the call without résumé or sermon. By this time, we had three children: Heide, Keith, and Monique.

I received my doctor of ministry degree from Drew University in Madison, New Jersey, in 1991.

Ego Integrity vs. Despair Maturity (age 65+)

I served over thirty-two years as senior pastor of the Mount Sinai Baptist Church in Brooklyn before retiring as pastor emeritus in 2016.

There were times I felt like giving up. During this period, my only son, Keith, my oldest daughter, Heide, two sisters, two brothers, father and mother died This was a very trying time in my life. Then I remembered how I had encouraged others to stay strong in face of crises. I've always believed that nothing was outside the realm of possibility with Him, no matter what things I might not know or could not see. The difficulties and struggles along the way are part of the landscape we all encounter on the journey to the Promised Land.

During my journey, I have come to crossroads that have been difficult to navigate, but there was always that motivation to go forward. As God continued to guide and direct, He pointed out the desired route.

From the Union of Two Eleven were born

FAMILY PHOTO

Chapter 2
The Relevance of Historical Perspective

I am deeply convinced that any pastor who wants to effectively lead a congregation should know as much as possible about its DNA. This includes its history, goals, and mission. Having this information greatly enhances the ability to evaluate the needs and direction that God is leading the congregation during this critical period of transition. It's also an opportunity to get a sense of the direction the congregation is moving. Of paramount importance is knowing the atmosphere of board meetings and the relationship between members. For example, is there mutual respect among board members? Marshall Shelly summarizes this importance of the atmosphere of the board:

> The atmosphere of the board meeting itself is an excellent gauge of the church's health. Do board members pray for one another? Do they take time to find out one another's worries and joys? Time spent in personal ministry at the beginning of a board meeting time well spent. An unwritten agenda item at every healthy board meeting is "encouraging each other."[5]

The roots of the Mount Sinai Baptist Church, which I pastored for more than thirty-two years, extend deep into the fertile soil of African tradition. Crafting a ministry model for pastoral care is best viewed through the lens of the Afro-American tradition, which graphically portrays its *sitz en leben*.

The brief historical account that follows, informs our understanding of the relevance of the current ministry model under consideration.

Without a doubt, slave trade has had a debilitating effect on the lives of black Americans. Albert J. Raboteau, author of *Slave Religion*, underscores the devastating experience that Africans endured:

> The enslavement of an estimated ten million Africans
> Over a period of almost four centuries in the Atlantic
> Slave trade was a tragedy of such scope that it is
> Difficult to imagine, much less comprehend. When these
> Africans were brought to slavery in the mines, plantation,
> And households of the New World, they were torn away from the
> Political, social, and cultural systems that had ordered their lives.
> Tribal and linguistic groups were broken up, either on the coasts of
> Africa or in the slave pens across the Atlantic. Most brutal of all, the
> Exigencies of the slave trade did not allow the preservation of family
> Or kingship ties.[6]

Another historian describes this crisis in almost the same terms. E. Franklin Frazier concludes in his book *The Negro Church in America*:

> The enslavement of the Negro not only destroyed the traditional African system of kinship and other forms of organized social life, but it made insecure and precarious the most elementary form of social life which tended to sprout anew, so to speak, on American soil—the family.[7]

Despite this attempt to eradicate all forms of African culture, African beliefs and customs persisted and were transmitted by slaves to their descendants. One of the most durable and adaptable constituents of the slave's culture, linking African past with American present, was their religion. The only institution that gave the slave any status was the black church. It was the only institution among the Negroes that started in the African forest and survived slavery. The church preserved the remnants of African tribal life under the leadership of the priest and medicine man. C. Eric Lincoln highlights the significance of the black church in providing resources for survival:

> The church was the black man's government, his social club, his secret order, his Espionage system, his political party, and his impetus to freedom and revolution. It provided the counterpart of the "Weltanschauung" in the African culture from which he had been separated.[8]

The history of the struggles of black people can be characterized as very stormy. We have survived the middle passage. The flame flickered, and we have survived slavery. We have survived the deadly arbitrariness of Jim Crow and the hypocritical hatefulness of Northern discrimination. As one searches for reasons for this indefatigable spirit, it is to be found within the black church.

On September 1919, when black congregations had begun to spring up in both the South and the North, this congregation was born. From 1919 to 1984, it was led by three pastors. I assumed pastoral leadership as the fourth pastor from 1984 until July 31, 2016.

I was charged with the responsibility of providing creative ministry to a congregation whose life was more than a building composed of just wood, brick, wire, and glass. Conscious of its rich heritage, I realized the unique challenge of giving directions and leadership to a people whose building housed their trials and tribulations, joys and sorrows, happiness and griefs, successes and failures.

An additional aspect important to this congregation is its surroundings. It is here we present a bird's-eye view of Brooklyn, which has been called the borough of churches. Brooklyn was often the final settling place for those who came to New York in the nineteenth and twentieth centuries. Its residents have roots in many Latin countries, in all parts of the African continent, in Europe's east and west, in the Caribbean, and in Central and South America, as well as a growing number of Asian nations. Kings County's seventy square miles hold more diversity than any place in America except the United Nations. There is presently a critical, growing need in the community for more services as the number of poor continues to increase. Being acutely aware of the plight of the homeless, poor, and undereducated masses, we can make a difference. This is the nature of our mission in the world. In this area there are more crack houses than church houses. Crime in the community is increasing. Members are often afraid to come to church for fear for their lives. Members' cars are sometimes stolen out of the church's parking lot while attending service. Members are plagued by extreme denial and deprivation—socially, physically, and economically. Drug and alcohol abuse have afflicted either a church member, his or her family, or a relative. Unemployment, substandard housing, and a host of other social ills affect the community. There is a very high expectation for pastoral counseling and involvement in these crisis situations. At times one can sense a great deal of pain and anxiety.

Creating a ministry model of pastoral care and counseling is therefore a response to liberation and transformation of a people who are facing the challenge of the existential dilemma. It is action directed to help people step out of ruts and into the mainstream of society; to give food and shelter when it is needed, and to stand up for the rights of those who are unable to stand alone. It should be noted that this care is even more desperately needed among oppressed peoples, even though the literature and resources among them would seem to be limited.

Short-term crisis care is the church's response and an ongoing, vital part of the Christian ministry today. It is a perpetual concern to meet the needs of persons from all walks of life. Because the caring of souls is so basic, a primary objective is to enable each trainee to increase his or her ability to listen, understand, and respond to the needs of others, as well as to recognize, acknowledge, and deal with one's own personal gifts and limitations. The following objectives will be emphasized:

A. To gain basic skills in the care of souls within the Mount Sinai Church. Included are emphases on the art of communication in pastoral care, the church as the context of such care, and strategies for short-term care.

B. To gain more insight into the role of the lay person in relation to other helping professions. Is there a uniqueness to laity involvement in the crisis situation? What are the limits and possibilities of lay care, and how does this relate to other professionals in the healing arts? The crisis situations to be discussed will include: AIDS, drugs, alcohol, depression, and terminal illness.

C. Developing aggressive, bold leadership that will mobilize the laity to effectively respond to the myriad of crises becomes a vital concern for ministry. This objective is highlighted by Patricia Benner:

> Caring ministering in concrete specific ways to concrete others, is a profoundly sacred, hopeful Christian practice. The biblical injunction to love one another, to give food to the hungry and water to the thirsty provides the basis for caring practices. The Church is called to restore the appreciation and value of caring practices. We feel cared for when we are treated as members and participants in a community of care and responsibility and we feel at risk when we are treated as merely numbers.[9]

Chapter 3
Professional Preparation

One of the fundamental principles in initiating and implementing the crisis team ministry is to begin with a purpose. This purpose should be rooted and grounded in the rich soil of the Great Commission, "Go therefore and make disciples of all nations, baptizing them in the name of the Father an of the Son and of the Holy Spirit, teaching them to observe all that I have commanded you; and lo, I am with you always to the close of the age" (Matthew 28:19–20 RSV).

This Great Commission should serve as a road marker to ensure we are all headed in the right direction and that we have everyone who is supposed to be with us on board.

Caregiver Selection

Caution should be used at the outset to avoid making the selection based on filling a number requirement. Neither should it be to stack the deck with those possessing exceptional educational qualifications, although several of the team members were trained professionals in their daily lives. Some of the team participants were currently working as social workers in various fields such as child care agencies and drug and alcohol rehabilitation centers. Since my wife was a psychiatric social work supervisor, she provided invaluable resources as a team member. Some participants were recovering drug and substance abusers with no more formal schooling than a high school diploma. This heterogenous mix of professionals and nonprofessionals worked to a great advantage.

Recovering drug and substance abusers worked very well with persons holding social work degrees.

One of the key issues that has to be dealt with, other than the frequency and number of sessions, is candidate qualifications. One of the prerequisites for being selected should be the caregiver's basic understanding of his or her call to service. Prayerfully seeking the will of the Lord, interview each trainee and ascertain their reasons for believing themselves to be called to this particular ministry. One of the leading questions should be "What qualities do you think someone ought to have be a good caregiver?" Keep in mind that many people in the congregation do not have the capacity to help others, just as there are many people who do not have the capacity to design computers or perform surgery. Each job requires certain kinds of people with certain kinds of talents. The selection process must also be guided by the fact that among the kinds of people who are not good helpers are those who are interested in knowing about people rather than in serving them; those who are impelled by strong personal needs to control, to feel superior, or to be liked; those who have solved problems similar to the problems of the people in need of help but have forgotten what it cost them to do so; and those who are primarily interested in retributive justice and moralizing.

There are certain qualities, attitudes, and approaches toward life that are found to an uncommon degree among good caregivers. They are identified by Compton & Galaway and served as a guideline for the selection of the fifteen caregivers. There are six qualities that are seen as central to effective caregiver functioning:

1. Nurturing People: The most effective caregivers usually consider themselves as living, growing, developing people who are deeply involved in the process of becoming. They do not exclude themselves from the human condition but view all people, including themselves, as engaged in problem solving. Not only are they unafraid of life, they frankly enjoy the process of being alive with all the struggle that this may involve. They find change and growth exciting rather than threatening. Their anxiety and tension are at an optimum level, so they are free to take on new experiences. They do not need to be right to defend where they are. Most of the qualities that will be discussed are directly related to this quality.

2. **Creativity:** This means originality, expressiveness, and imagination. It involves an unusual amount of openness to all experiences of life, the ability to hold knowledge in suspension, a never-satisfied curiosity, and a lack of identification with conformist opinion.

3. **Self-Awareness:** This quality has to do with flexibility, a sense of humor, a readiness to learn, an acceptance of one's limitations, and an openness—all of which are important to caregiving.

4. **Desire to Help:** Simply put, this is a commitment to oneself, rather than to others, because it must be our desire, be related to us, and be a commitment to ourselves. It is this commitment that gives one the courage to know oneself and the willingness to risk oneself in the service of others. The Good Samaritan did not stop and give first aid to the man beaten and left in a ditch, but he was willing to risk his life in the service of another. The Good Samaritan was the first of a series of sermons I preached to call attention to the project in caregiving.

5. **Courage:** Caregivers must be willing to assume the risks of failing to help; of becoming involved in difficult, emotionally charged situations that they do not know how to handle; of having their comfortable world and ways of operating upset; of being blamed and abused; of being constantly involved in the unpredictable, and perhaps being physically threatened.

6. **Sensitivity:** Our methods of sharing ourselves completely with others are awkward and imperfect even when we are committed to that sharing. For troubled people, the ability to share themselves and their situations is incredibly more difficult because of all their feelings about their problems and about themselves as people with problems as well as the threat of the unknown in the helping process. Therefore, the worker who would help needs a capacity for feeling and sensing, for knowing the inner state of others without specific clues. The crucial factor in this selection process

was that there needed to be some common ground between persons facing life crises and the purpose of the program. Whether this purpose has been defined broadly or narrowly, each member of the team must find some connection between a personal sense of urgency and the care involved.

Chapter 4
Biblical Models for a Caring Community

During the implementation of this ministry it was made clear that training of lay persons made full use of the untapped resources that reside in the congregation. It is maximizing the present ministry. Training persons to be efficient caregivers is a vital link in the life and ministry of any congregation. The ministry of the laity is essentially a ministry to persons in need. The training is grounded on the comprehension of the concept "Priesthood of All Believers." It further instills confidence and the conviction that even the simplest acts of caring are commissioned by God. Lay persons not only need to be trained in the skills of helping people confront hazardous and difficult life experiences, they also should be aware of some of the biblical models for a caring community.

In any type of Christian caring—whether it be individual, marital, or familial—knowledge and application of biblical methods are essential. One way to develop a biblical approach is to study the life of Jesus and His relationships with others. The way He ministered to others is a model for all who are involved in the helping ministry. In the study of the ministry of Jesus, it is evident that He demonstrated characteristics that left little doubt that He cared for those who were the recipients of His warmth, understanding, acceptance, and belief in their ability to change and mature.

An important observation that can be made of Jesus's ministry is that He worked with people through a process. He spent time helping them work through life's difficulties. He saw people not only with their problems but with their potentials and hopes as well. A basic characteristic of Jesus's method was His compassion for others.

> "I have compassion on the multitude, because they have now been with me three days, and have nothing to eat."—Mark 8:2 (KJV)

> "And Jesus, when he came out, saw much people, and was moved with compassion toward them, because they were as sheep not having a shepherd; and he began to teach them many things."—Mark 6:34 (KJV)

His concern was to alleviate suffering and meet the needs of the people. A hallmark of Jesus's ministry of caring was also acceptance as seen in John 4, John 8, and Luke 19. When Jesus met the woman at the well, He accepted her as she was without judging her. He accepted the woman caught in adultery, and Zacchaeus, the dishonest tax collector. Individuals were Jesus's top priority. They were assisted in discovering their personal worth. Discernment was another quality that may be seen in the example of Nicodemus coming to Jesus during the night. The reasons for Nicodemus requesting a private audience at this time are uncertain. However, Jesus discerned in Nicodemus a real need and confronted him with the need to experience the new birth. Jesus also sought to have people accept responsibility for turning from their present condition. In John 5, He responded to the man at the pool of Bethesda by saying, "Wilt thou be made whole?" In other words, "Do you really want to get well? Do you want to be healed? Do you want to change?" This procedure was to get the man to accept responsibility for remaining sick or being made well.

Another biblical example of Jesus's model of caring was that He spent an enormous amount of time with the burdened, the disturbed, and the sick. His parable of the shepherd who left the ninety-nine to help the one lost sheep showed His concern for the individual in need. His words, "Those are well having no need of a physician, but those who are sick" (Mark 2:17) indicates unmistakably the orientation of His ministry. In describing His ministry as he quoted from Isaiah 61, highlighted is the fact that He came to proclaim release for prisoners and recovery of sight for the blind; to let the broken victims go free (Luke 4:18 NEB).

Summary

Persons whom Jesus encountered were either in a crisis or getting ready to be hit by one. There were times He treated them differently based on the individual cases. He approached each case with a basic philosophy that was not solely biblical or theological; He used everyday experience and knowledge of human nature to diagnose the case and provide the prescription. He had compassion; He confronted persons; He broke the barriers of separation. He met people where they were and treated them there. Since the church has a long history of ministering to persons in need, combining the biblical with the theoretical and practical becomes a very significant model for this ministry of caring.

Chapter 5
Theological Foundations

The Response of the Church to Persons Facing Crises

The church, from early times, has always been a healing community. However, its response can be a blemish on the body of faith or a beacon bringing the bright blessings of hope and love. Serving more than half a century in ministry, it has become clear to me that persons in the throes of pain and loss come yearning for some tangible nourishment, some sign from the church that they are neither alone in suffering nor forsaken. The relevance of the church's response is underscored by Blundall:

> The church of today, unlike other institutions in society, finds itself in a unique position in responding to the needs of persons experiencing life's crises. consequently, there is a growing concern to discover what role it must assume in alleviating the ever-increasing needs born out of the character of a culture in crises. Within the church community there are many voices which come from members in different stages of faith and crisis. The church cannot afford to neglect its task in grappling with the life and death issues which its members must experience. Families in crises who feel torn by the pressure and the pain of either hanging on or letting go of their dreams and their way of life need basic training from the Church. Every Church is plagued by an ugly

> scene of cripples at the steps of its entrance. (cf Acts 3:1–11).[10]

In other words, the church does not have an option in its ministry to such crises but is challenged to provide creative and purposeful ministry to meet the needs of those for whom no one seems to care. It must not only be efficient in the diagnosis of the illness, but it must become the embodiment of the Negro spiritual's declaration, "There is a balm in Gilead."

There are several reasons why the church can be unique in responding to those who are suffering. First, the example that our Lord set for the church was one in which He cared about people and suffered when they did. Consequently, the church assumed this healing ministry, so there was a time when those who were experiencing suffering and pain would look to the church for healing. However, as the scientific world began to flourish, people started looking to the medical profession for healing, and interest in the early church as a healing agent diminished. This shift is noted by Benner:

> Fifty years ago the Church was visibly involved in the work of caring practices and healing communities and established many hospitals. So strong was the call to be a healing community that religious opportunities established their own hospitals (e.g. The Presbyterian hospital, The Baptist Hospital, The Beth Israel, and many others.) When the understanding of hospitals switched from healing community to that of scientific-technical "repair" shops selling goods and services, the link between the Church and the hospital weakened. The centrality of caring practices and restoration through healing communities has been hidden by the technical scientific self- understanding. caring practices has now become a business driven by the culture and ethos of competitive "product lines." Person, body and community have artificially been separated.[11]

In recent years, the healthcare profession has discovered that an overwhelming demand has been placed on its resources, and it is unable to keep up with the pace of providing quality care. Cutbacks have been necessary, causing some facilities, which so many people depended on, to close up shop. These conditions have affected the quality care that used to be a vital part of the day-to-day operation in the average caring community and has some serious implications for the development of lay visitation. For example, a person who is hospitalized for the first time and then sent home long before recuperation is complete is placed in a dilemma. He or she must begin scouting around to find someone to take over where the hospital left off. This ministry becomes even more crucial with the devastating blow of the AIDS epidemic that has hit our communities. The result is that society has experienced a great loss in the appreciation and value of caring. It is here that the church can provide very meaningful and caring assistance to individuals who have become victims of this lost art. Based on this situation, the church must be involved in a caring way.

Secondly, there is no other institution that has been commissioned and empowered to be engaged in the redemptive activity of rebuilding broken and run-down lives of those in our church and community. Additionally, the injunction to love one another, to give food to the hungry and water to the thirsty, provides the basis for caring practices. It is true that one can feel cared for when he or she is treated as a member and participant in a community of care and responsibility but can feel at risk when treated as merely a thing or object. The church is unique in its role here because it is that community that is most central in nurturing Christian faith in daily life. However, this does not discredit the fact that family and friends, weekend conferences, and national programs on the ministry of the laity are instrumental in stimulating individuals to connect faith to daily life. But the ongoing community of believers is where each of us looks for meaning; seeks inspiration, forgiveness, and renewal; and shares our joys and struggles with one another.

A major emphasis in the development of this project is supported by literature that suggests the church is not an end but rather the means through which God works in the world, where we gather around Word and sacrament, learn of God's Word, and experience fellowship and support. Also, we are God's people in ministry to one another and to the world, and the mandate of the church is for the community of faith, in the midst of the world, to serve the world.

Nelson Vos raises a pivotal question as it relates to the relationship of the church in its ministry to members:

> What does a congregation look like which takes seriously the ministry of its members in daily life? More theologically, how is the Church to be understood? Such questions get to the root of the matter, for ministry in daily life is one of the most obvious ways of the presence of the Church in the world. What is needed therefore at a minimum within the local congregation is an intentional effort 1) To recognize that daily life is the primary setting for the exercise of our calling. 2) To affirm the variety of God-given gifts among us. 3) To equip persons more effectively for their ministry in the world and 4) To support one another as we respond to God's presence in our lives.[12]

Engaging in a ministry of caregiving is a way to put into practice our presence in the world and ensure that this presence is authenticated by a clear understanding of the four standards that we reiterate: (1) The recognition that daily life is the primary setting for the exercise of our calling; (2) Affirming the variety of God-given gifts among us; (3) Equipping persons to be more effective for their ministry in the world; and (4) supporting one another as we respond to God's presence in our lives. The image of the church as an army has a tremendous impact on our own understanding of the nature and function of the church. Bufford and Buckler give a very apt and descriptive analogy of the church in terms of its nature and function in God's army:

> The analogy of the church as an army is one with considerable biblical basis. Believers are urged to arm themselves (Ephesians 6:10–17; Romans 13:12;

> 2 Corinthians 6:7) to fight a good fight (1 Timothy 1:18, 6:12), to serve single mindedly as good soldiers (2 Timothy 2:4). The Bible itself is likened to a two-edged sword (Hebrews 4:12). We have an adversary who must be resisted at the east of suffering so that we are not destroyed (1 Peter 5:8–10). A modern army has many branches: infantry, artillery, air corps, intelligence, police, doctrine and training, supply, transportation, construction, medical, and many other. The structure of an army is designed so that each branch carries out its own unique mission in support of the overall effort. When any branch fails in its mission the whole military effort suffers. The same is true of the Christian army.[13]

The army metaphor, in addition to others, provides a significant framework for articulating the nature, purpose, and essence of the church as it responds to the needs of persons in the grip of severe crises. The church of the New Testament must never forget its role as the army of God. Paul urged Timothy to share in suffering as a good soldier of Christ Jesus.

In many ways the Christian army functions like a counterinsurgency force—there are no front lines, and the enemy is everywhere and uses unpredictable methods and strategies. The wear and tear of the battle is manifested in many ways. In the military context, group cohesion has been found to be one of the most important factors in the prevention of psychological breakdown on the battlefield. Current research on the nature of the church consistently reveals two major factors associated with positive response to persons who become wounded in life's battles: meaning and purpose in life, and involvement in an effective social support system. It has been demonstrated that that a well-functioning Christian church is an ideal context in which these may be provided. The church, through its development of programs such as crisis intervention and family life ministry, affords the small group cohesion and social support network that are important factors in mitigating the effects of stress on the individual.

The motto of the US Army's medical corps is to conserve the fighting strength of the army. While the focus is primarily on function, it is widely recognized that freedom from pain and suffering enables a soldier to function more effectively. In a similar fashion, the medical corps of the Christian army needs to be concerned with maintaining the effectiveness of each member. This includes relief from the pain and suffering, both physical and psychological, for those injured in spiritual warfare.

The medical corps of a modern army operates at several levels or echelons. The battlefield medic works alongside the combatants, providing emergency first aid on the battleground. At the battalion aid station, intermediate care is provided and triage decisions are made regarding the nature, extent, and urgency of any additional care needed. Those able to do so are returned to the battle; others are evacuated either to a field hospital for further treatment with the expectation of early return to combat or to a general hospital for more extended care.

In the church, the ministrations of the battlefield medic may be analogous to the comfort, encouragement, and exhortation of a fellow believer. The Christian caregiver in the local church may serve much like the battalion aid station, providing crisis care, evaluation, and helping to decide the need for further assistance.

The body of Christ is another image that facilitates our understanding of the church in the world and its position of responding to needs of persons. We now address this matter.

The Body of Christ

In developing a ministry of caring, it is important to be clear in our notion of the church as the body of Christ. The view should not be one based on abstract terms, but on ways that describe the people of God as extensions of Christ who are placed by Christ in history. The concept "body of Christ" describes the new and unique nature of this people of God.

In Hellenistic language it was common to express with the word *body* the unity of anything that consisted of various members (e.g., the state, the cosmos, a speech, a melody, a vine).

The church as the body of Christ in the world is challenged to respond to the estrangement and alienation of people in the community.

The church has a responsibility in the reconciliation of a world that's populated by lost souls for whom no one seems to care. This project challenges the membership of Mount Sinai to actively engage in the life-giving function of the body of Christ.

The significance of this mission is highlighted by Kung:

> On its journey out into the world the church has a mission, a commission, a task, a ministry which it must fulfill in the present and which is always given to it by the present, this is what fulfills it, giving it reality and purpose. What presents itself constantly to the Church in the present is nothing other than God's grace, under which the Church lives and which very day brings anew. It is this grace which helps the Church to overcome all the anxieties of the present, all the shortcomings, all the doubts, all the care, all the hopelessness, all its illusions that it can redeem itself, all the wretchedness of the Church and the world.[13]

The body image of the church provides insight of great importance in the comprehension of the relationship between Christ and the church. From Him, the whole body, supplied and built from joints and ligaments, attains a growth that is of God. He continually distributes in His body, that is, in the church, gifts of ministries through which, by His own power, we serve one another unto salvation so that, carrying out the truth in love, we may through all things grow up into He who is our head.

The body of Christ is seen as the people of God, as spiritual creation and in concrete historical terms. Closely associated with the body image is community. Our present task is to define its relationship to the ministry of responding to persons in need.

Community

A considerable amount of the literature describes the church as a community. It is essential to be clear in the comprehension of the biblical and theological meaning of community as it pertains to the church. In his letter to the Colossians, Paul writes:

> In him (Christ) everything in heaven and on earth was created, not only things visible but also the invisible orders of thrones, sovereignties, authorities and powers: the whole universe has been created through him and for him and he exists before everything and all things are held together in him. Through him God chose to reconcile the whole universe to himself making peace through the shedding of his blood upon the cross—to reconcile all things whether on earth or in heaven through him alone.[14]

The image here is one of profound harmony and systemic interconnectedness emerging out of a sense of meaning and obedience. When this interconnectedness is experienced in the human sphere, we have what is called community. The biblical word that most fully expresses this theologically is *shalom*, sometimes translated from the Hebrew as "peace." Shalom is an all-encompassing word covering the many relationships of life and expressing a vision of what the Israelites conceived as the idea of what life was intended by God to be. In defining shalom, commentators use such words as wholeness, totality, well-being, and the absence of violence or misfortune.

In describing what this experience of Christian community is like, the New Testament uses the word *koinonia* or quite literally "sharing" in partnership or fellowship. As the author of the first Epistle of John writes: "If we walk in the light we share together a common life."

The original Greek word *koinonia* suggests deep and genuine fellowship or sharing. In the New Testament, Paul speaks of the participation and mutual fellowship among believers stemming from the relationship of each individual believer in Christ. Within this fellowship or partnership, there is an experience of belonging, which is important because in crisis, we need the support of others. This can be facilitated through koinonia possible today among people who come together from all walks of life to share in one central concern.

Another dimension of koinonia is partnership: All Christians are partners in Christ. Even in the counseling relationship, the counselor and the counselee give and receive from each other. Koinonia is always active, never passive or stagnant. It is spontaneous and uncontrived. It exists in relationships where sharing and reaching out occur. This sharing and reaching out was emphasized from beginning to end of planning this model of caregiving at Mount Sinai.

The potential for koinonia exists with all people. Out of it comes trust, and as a result of trust, people will more freely go to one another for help in crises. Whenever koinonia exists within a Christian community, pastoral care naturally becomes a function of the total congregation.

A key concept that clarifies the meaning of the church as a community is that the focus is not on making life pleasant but participating in what is fundamental to the redemptive activity of God. The foundational structure upon which this program is based is the reconciliation of the human family as we exist in relationship to one another and to the created order that sustains us. It is this redemptive activity of God, focused sharply in the person of Jesus Christ, that takes seriously overcoming the separation that exists between individuals, groups, and structures in society that pit nation against nation, race against race, man against woman, father against son, mother against daughter. Within the community, there is recognition of the reality of sin, that fundamental state of separation that touches all aspects of our existence. However, there is the belief that available to this koinonia is access to power that breaks through loneliness and isolation and calls us into relationship with others. When anyone is united with Christ, there is a new world; the old order has gone, and a new order has already begun (2 Corinthians 5:17). The image of community becomes a reservoir of hope as it continues in the redemptive activity of God. Holtmann articulates the hope that is generated by this community:

> Here Christian communities and group too, can become kind of Noah's Ark for men (persons) (author's insertion) in their social estrangement. They become islands of genuine co-humanity and of authentic life in the rough sea of circumstances which the ordinary man (person) can after all do nothing to alter.

The community of faith is that context in which hope resides, and the person who is experiencing a crisis is thereby provided with a certain compensation for the economic and technical forces of destruction. The community is formed and continues its existence by a story. Jesus told His disciples: "Heaven and earth will pass away: my words will never pass away" (Mark 13:31). Ours is a story whose words and deeds are empowered by the Word. It is a story that begins at the world's creation; climaxes in the life, death, and resurrection of Jesus Christ; and propels us through the church into the future as a people who have experienced a new order of human existence. "And be assured, I am with you always, to the end of time" (Matthew 28:20).

Chapter 6
Social Science Foundations

Systems Theories

Increasingly, our highly trained and dedicated professional help institutions have begun to recognize that they alone cannot provide the resources and social supports that are so vital to the well-being of the communities in which we live. There is an invisible partnership of which they are unaware; it is a web woven by a combination of neighbors, friends, coworkers, relatives, volunteer agencies, and human service organizations.

We use helping networks to get assistance for daily life problems such as depression, getting better jobs, obtaining education, dealing with retirement, crime in the community, family planning, and youth problems. Knowledge of how people deal with personal family problems and crises, especially outside the parameters of professional agencies, has been the concern of much research in recent years.

This literature has given much attention to the importance of support networks for helping individuals in crises. These studies have suggested that strong support systems are important for maintaining an individual's equilibrium in the time of crisis to facilitate growth.

The purpose of this section is to review the nature, role, and dynamics of support networks in relation to persons in crises. It is important to understand some of the theories used in the social work field as they inform our understanding of the nature of the person-environment interrelatedness and the person-situation transactions. It is here that we examine the ecological systems theory as a conceptual framework, which, according to Compton and Galaway shifts attention from the cause and effect relationship between paired variables (does the environment cause the person to behave in a certain way, or does the person affect the environment in a certain way?) to the person/situation as an interrelated whole.

A system is defined by Compton and Galaway as:

> A whole, a unit, composed of people and their interactions, including their relationships. Each person in the system is related to at least some others in the system in a more or less stable way within a period and space. Although a system should be viewed as a constantly changing whole that is always in process of movement toward its goals, its parts are assumed to interact in a more or less patterned way within a stable structure at any particular point in time. Within a system, something is always going on and that something is not random, it is an effort to achieve the system's goals.[15]

One of the great benefits in approaching intervention from the perspective of the ecological systems theory is that it relays to the caregivers a theoretical base on which to develop a model of a much-expanded repertoire of interventive action. Furthermore, it helps one understand the concept of the open system. According to the systems theory, closed systems do not interact with any other system; they neither accept input from them nor convey output to them. When systems are closed, they are said to have a quality called entropy. What this means is that closed systems over time tend toward less differentiation of their elements (all elements begin to be alike) and thus there is a loss of organization and effective function.

A striking example of this is the problems that are found in children of families that have rigid, closed boundaries and do not permit input from other systems in the community. All social systems must be open to input from other systems with which they interact if they are to grow and develop. In order to understand the concepts of the support systems as they relate to the healing process, we are obliged to consider some of the conceptual models that have been develop by Gerald Caplan. The focus of his models is not so much on the causes of mental disorders in populations but on the health-promoting forces at the person-to-person and social levels that enable people to master challenges and strains in their lives. The healing force of the local church can be a tremendous power base for helping people to constructively deal with crises. A large body of human and animal research has recently been reviewed demonstrating that increased population density, rapid social change, and social disorganization enhances susceptibility to disease. This research supports the hypothesis that:

> The circumstances in which increased susceptibility to disease would occur would be those in which, for a variety of reasons, individuals are not receiving any evidence (feedback) that their actions are leading to desirable and/or anticipated consequences.[16]

Caplan concludes that:

> The harmful effect of absent or confusing feedback in a general population may be reduced in the case of those individuals who are effectively embedded in their own smaller social networks which provide them with consistent communications of what is expected of them, supports and assistance with tasks, evaluation of their performance, and appropriate rewards. If these are not provided by society as a whole, they can be obtained from a social subgroup.[17]

Another concept that gives additional insight to our understanding is that people have a variety of specific needs that demand satisfaction through enduring interpersonal relationships, such as love and affection, intimacy that provides the freedom to easily express feelings, validation of personal identity and worth, satisfaction of nurturance and dependency, help with tasks, and support in handling emotion and controlling impulses.

Most people develop and maintain a sense of well-being by involving themselves in a range of relationships such as marriage, parenthood, and other forms of loving and intimate ties. They include friendships and relationships with colleagues at work; membership in religious congregations; and social, cultural, political, and recreational affiliations.

Implications of Systems Theory for the Black Church

A key factor in the design of this ministry is based on the concept of support systems as it relates to the black church. It was the black church that, in the words of Wimberly, emerged out of an environment of slavery because of the severity of the psychosocial and spiritual needs of oppressed black persons. Black persons needed to experience a sense of identity in the midst of slavery as an inhumane institution. A spiritual requisite was the need for the black slave to find a sense of meaning and purpose in life within the context of cruel servitude.

Specifically, systems theory as it relates to the training of lay persons has provided a great sense in understanding the value of collective identity and human wholeness. Throughout the sessions, individual members of the team should share their feelings of emotional and spiritual support as they experience the compensation of such support. Team members should come from varied backgrounds. This will help the training to be both therapeutic and redemptive. Members will experience the joy of a loving community, where caring for one another and mutual concern is top priority.

Crisis Theory

The major figure in the systematic development of crisis theory within psychiatry was Gerald Caplan, who, with Erich Lindemann, established a community mental health program in the Cambridge, Massachusetts, area in 1946. Much of what has been done in this field during the last decade has been an elaboration of, or at least somehow in response to, Caplan's work. A crisis, according to Caplan, arises out of some change in a person's life space that produces a modification of one's relationship with other and/or one's perceptions of oneself. Such change may come about relatively slowly, as a result of rather normal and inevitable experiences of growing and developing physically and socially, or quite rapidly, as a result of some unforeseen and traumatic event. These two concepts have been differentiated by referring to them as developmental and accidental crises. Erik Erikson has elaborated the former in detail. He proposes that life is to be thought of as a series of eight stages, each of which has significance in and of itself but also contributes to or detracts from the achievement of the goal of integrity, which he has designated the positive goal of the final stage. Each of these stages has its task and outcome characterized by contrasting terms—one emphasizing the positive need and the positive outcome if the need is successfully met, and the other a possible negative result. For example, the series of stages of childhood are basic trust versus mistrust, autonomy versus shame and doubt, initiative versus guilt, and industry versus inferiority. The needs and conflicts of adolescence are penetratingly and helpfully elaborated in the discussion of identity versus self-diffusion.

Adulthood consists progressively of intimacy versus self-absorption, generativity versus stagnation, and finally, integrity versus despair. It is clear that if a person is to accomplish the tasks and have the needs of one of these stages adequately met, it is important that basic trust has been established in the very first stage and that the outcome of each successive stage be more on the positive side than on the negative. Since specific procedures of helping are directly related to the particular dynamics and behavior of a given situation, it is essential that there be a precise definition of crisis. One of the major problems or difficulties is that there are numerous definitions.

Since ministers do in fact deal with a broad spectrum of human conditions, it would be useful to point to some of the most usual situations to which the word *crisis* is applied. Six categories of crisis have been developed by Baldwin:[18]

1. Dispositional. The person feels distressed (anxiety, anger, hopelessness, etc.) as a result of a particular external problematic situation, in which the distress can be immediately removed by direct means: referral to physician to receive medical treatment or to an agency to receive food or be assisted to find housing

by the giving of information, by medical or psychological education, or by administrative action, such as the restoring of a job.

2. Anticipated Life Transitions: These are usually normal situations a person knows are going to happen and over which the person may or may not have control: a housing move, a job change, becoming a parent.

3. Sudden Traumatic Stress: Here a specific external event triggers a very rapid reaction of distress, usually involving extreme anxiety or some amount of depression, or both, and some breakdown in functioning. There may have been the loss of a job; the loss of a person by death separation, or divorce; or some other event perceived as threatening.

4. Maturational/Developmental: Because life goes on, a person is required to attempt to make adjustments, with successful moves being in the direction greater maturity. If there are developmental issues not dealt with adequately in the past, there is greater difficulty in making the new adjustment. Significant issues that keep coming up are those that have to do with dependency, values, emotional and sexual intimacy, self-discipline, the sense and exercise of power.

5. Psychopathological: These crises result primarily from the reactivation of unresolved earlier severe failures in maturation or critical losses and usually result in behavior to which the term psychotic would be properly applied.

6. Psychiatric Emergencies: This category refers to the first helping contacts of persons who are becoming psychotic or who are suicidal, homicidal, or are behaving in other extreme ways. For the purpose of our training, those crises that have been listed in the third category—Sudden Traumatic Stress—will be referred to throughout as situational crises.

The Situational Crisis: Description and Dynamics

A situational crisis differs from a developmental crisis primarily in the source of stress and the element of time. There is a more rapid modification of perception of one's self and one's world, frequently including relationships with other persons and usually initiated by some type of personal loss perceived as a threat to self. Along with this form of external event, or in place of it, there may be some other sudden change in a situation that challenges one's self-concept or sense of identity. According Rapport[19], "There are three sets of interrelated factors that can produce a state of crisis: (1) a hazardous event which poses some threat; (2) a threat to instinctual need which is symbolically linked to earlier threats that resulted in vulnerability or conflict; (3) an inability to respond with adequate coping mechanisms (acute stage).

In crisis theory there is the assumption that a number of physical, psychosocial, and sociocultural needs contribute to the fundamental ego integrity of a person. Among the most important psychosocial needs are those that cluster around a person's relationship with others in and outside the family so that cognitive and emotional development are stimulated, the need for love and affection is met, behavioral guidelines are given, personal support is supplied, reality testing takes place, and opportunities are provided to work with others on tasks seen as significant. Physical illness often produces crisis, and two factors seem to be involved. One is the relationship between the concept of body image and the whole self. The first major step in the development of self is the infant's finally coming to the place where he or she can distinguish between what is outside the skin and what is inside, the delineation of the infant's own body, the setting it off from the rest of the world.

The full psychosocial self of the adult is preceded in time by the recognition of the physical self, and therefore the body image forms the foundation of and is incorporated into what later comes to be the total self. Thus, any change in or attack on the body is perceived to be an attack on one's whole self.

Curtis L. Whitney

Tenets of Crisis Intervention Theory

Crisis intervention (CI) is a widely used general interventive strategy for equipping persons to cope more effective with the myriad difficulties they encounter in this life. The key to understanding the strategy of crisis intervention evolves from the concept that when people are beset by a crisis, a potential exists for them to cope in ways that are either adaptive or maladaptive. According to CI theorists, crisis situations generally are limited to a period of four to eight weeks, during which people manage to achieve some degree of equilibrium equivalent to, lower than, or higher than the precrisis level of functioning. Life crises can thus be viewed as presenting potential threats that can permanently impair people's level of functioning or as painful challenges that embody opportunities for growth in personal strength and coping capacity. CI theory emphasizes the importance of intervening immediately to assist persons who are overwhelmed by crisis. Timely intervention is critical not only in preventing deterioration in functioning, but also to reach people when their defenses are low and their receptiveness to therapeutic intervention is greatest.

Most crisis intervention theorists accept the definition of a crisis as an upset in a steady state (state of equilibrium) that poses an obstacle to the fulfillment of important life goals. How people deal with personal family and collective problems and crises outside the parameters of professional agencies has been the concern of much research in recent years.

A crisis is stressful and disruptive and can adversely affect biological, psychological, and social functioning, which can produce disturbed emotions, impair motor functioning, and negatively impact ongoing behavior. Crisis situations have a subjective element based on people's perceptions and coping capacities. What is severely stressful and overwhelming for one person or family may be stressful but manageable for others.

Crisis situations are diverse. Most people would agree that natural disasters, death of a loved one, disabling or life-threatening illness or injury, cultural dislocation, or other drastic environmental changes—such as rape, life-threatening premature birth, adolescent out-of-wedlock pregnancy, sudden absence of a key family member, and other like events—usually pose a crisis to those involved.

Hazardous events can be experienced as a threat, challenge, or loss (Rappoport 1970). A threat (e.g., possibility of losing a job, spouse, home, reputation, or valued status) may involve anticipated loss of an individual's sense of integrity or autonomy and involves high anxiety and apprehension about a possible dreaded event in the future.

The hazardous event itself requires a solution that is new in relation to the individual's previous life experience. Many individuals are able to develop new solutions by means of the normal range of problem-solving mechanisms stemming from their general life experience and maturation and are thereby able to deal adequately with the hazardous event. Here the crisis care team can be very effective in helping individuals whose life experiences may be deficient and will not allow any new solution to come forth.

The hazardous event creates for the individual a problem in his or her current life situation, and others are unable to respond with appropriate solutions; therefore, the hazardous event and its sequel continue as a source of stress. The person experiencing the hazardous event may be too devastated to think of anything new. It is at this point that the caregiver can suggest a course of action that the individual probably could have thought of him- or herself but whose homeostatic balance was too weak to act appropriately. The problem can be conceived of as a threat, a loss, or a challenge. The threat may be to fundamental instinctual needs or to the person's sense of integrity. The loss may be actual or may be experienced as a state of acute deprivation. For each of these states, there is a major characteristic mode in which the ego tends to respond. A threat to need and integrity is met with anxiety. Loss or deprivation is met with depression. If the problem is viewed as a challenge, it is more likely to be met with a mobilization of energy and purposeful problem-solving activities.

Since the hazardous event may contain a threat to instinctual needs, it is likely to be linked with old threats to instinctual needs and to trigger unresolved or partially resolved unconscious conflicts. The previous failure may act as an additional burden in the present crisis. It has been observed by various investigators that during a crisis, memories of old problems that are linked symbolically to the present are stimulated and may spontaneously emerge into consciousness or can be uncovered and dealt with by relatively brief therapeutic intervention.

Due to the short time involved in crisis intervention, it is necessary to assess and alleviate peoples' distress. Objectives of the assessment involve determining the nature of the crisis situation, its significance to and impact on the person(s), factors or events that precipitated the crisis, adaptive capacities of the individual, and resources that can be tapped to alleviate the crisis situation.

These factors are crucial to formulating tasks that must subsequently be accomplished. Caregivers must determine the unique meaning of crisis situations to each individual. Determining the meaning and significance of precipitating events can be highly therapeutic. Bear in mind that the intense anxiety and emotionalism typically associated with crisis situations severely reduces a person's capacity to think rationally and analytically. Through exploring precipitating events and other factors that bear on people reactions, caregivers must enable persons to view their situations in a new perspective, which can foster hope for the future.

The nature of a crisis provides valuable clues to the sources of a person's distress. Losses leave people bereft of vital sources of emotional supplies and typically produce grieving reactions, leading to differing emotional reactions. A person who has been extremely dependent on a spouse may react to the spouse's death with grief but also with feelings of helplessness and hopelessness concerning his or her ability to manage independently. A person whose relationship to a deceased spouse or parent was ambivalent and conflictual may react to the death with feelings of guilt, hostility, or even relief.

Summary

Crisis intervention posits the concept that when an individual is faced with a crisis, one of two things happen. First, the potential is there to cope in a way that is adaptive or maladaptive. If the individual copes in ways that are adaptive, then new learning and new insight emerges, and the person experiences a higher level of performance. If the attempt to cope is maladaptive, then the individual's level of functioning becomes inadequate, and if intervention is not immediate, deterioration in functioning can result.

Chapter 7
Training Resources

Session 1 Preview

I. Introduction to the Doctor of Ministry Program

Step 1. Welcome/Getting Acquainted
- a. Introductions
  - (1) Personal Data
  - (2) Motivation for Involvement in Training
  - (3) Sharing of Helping or Being Helped in a Crisis

Step 2. Overview/Goals, Purpose
- a. Organization of Group
- b. Definition of Terms
- c. Skills Identification
  - (1) Listening
  - (2) Tuning In
  - (3) Empathic
  - (4) Bonding

Step 3. Dynamics

Step 4. Case Studies

Step 5. Discussion (Handout) and Wrap Up

Session 2: Building an Authentic Caring Ministry

II. The Role of the Caregivers

Step 1. Identifying Crisis Situations
Step 2. Helping Strategies for Crises Intervention
Step 3. Affirming Theological Foundations
Step 4. Toward a Biblical Model for a Caring Ministry
Step 5. Case Studies
Step 6. Summary

Session 3 Practical Aspects

III. Theoretical and Practical Understandings

Step 1. Guidelines for Making Referrals
Step 2. Crisis Theory
Step 3. Systems Theory
Step 4. Introduction to Black Pastoral Care
Step 5. Verbatims

Session 4 Applications

IV. Nurturing Persons in Christian Growth

Step 1. Tool of the Trade
Step 2. Care of Souls in the Black Church
Step 3. Intervention Techniques
Step 4. Discussion/Summary/Wrap Up

Session 5: Helping with Specific Crises (Part 1)

V. Practical Applications

Step 1. Alcoholism and Substance Abuse
Step 2. Role Play

Step 3. Discussion on Substance Abuse
Step 4. Sharing Stories
Step 5. Summary/Reflections

Session 6: Helping with Specific Crises (Part 2)

VI. Film Presentation

Step 1. Overview
Step 2. Film: *Family Trap*
Step 3. Discussion
Step 4. Summary

Session 7: Personal Growth

VII. Audio Cassette Presentation

Step 1. Working Through Personal Crisis
Step 2. Understanding Depression
Step 3. Discussion
Step 4. Summary

Session 8

VIII. Special Presentation

Step 1. HIV/AIDS Seminar
Step 2. Discussion
Step 3. Wrap Up

Commissioning Service for Trainees

Steps for Effective Listening

1. **Stop Talking**—you can't listen while you are talking.

2. **Empathize with the Other Person**—try to put yourself in his or her place so that you can see what he or she is trying to get at. With your posture, facial expressions, and nonverbal communication, attend carefully to what the person is saying.

3. **Ask Questions**—do this when you don't understand, when you need further clarification, when you want the person to like you, when you want to show that you are listening. But don't ask questions that will embarrass the person or make him or her feel inferior.

4. **Don't Give up Too Soon**—don't interrupt the other person; give him or her time to say what has to be said.

5. **Concentrate on What the Person Is Saying**—actively focus your attention on the person's words, ideas, and feelings related to your subject.

6. **Look at the Other Person**—his or her face, mouth, eyes, or hands all help the person communicate with you. Looking at the person will help you concentrate and make him or her feel that you are listening.

7. **Smile and Grunt Appropriately**—but don't overdo it.

8. **Leave Your Worldly Cares Behind**—try to leave your worries, your fears, and your problems outside the meeting room. They may prevent you from listening well.

9. **Control Your Anger**—try not to get angry at what the person is saying; your anger may prevent you from understanding the other's words or meaning.

10. **Get Rid of Distractions**—put down any papers, pencils, etc., you have in your hands; they may distract your attention.

11. **Get the Main Points**—concentrate on the main ideas and not the illustrative material: examples, stories, and statistics are important but are usually not the main points. Examine them only to see if they prove, support, or define the main ideas

12. **Share Responsibility for Communication**—only part of the responsibility rests with the speaker; you as the listener have an important part. Try to understand, and if you don't, ask for clarification.

13. **React to Ideas, Not to the Person**—don't let your personal reactions to the person influence your interpretation of what he or she says. The person's ideas may be good even if you don't like him or her as a person or the way he or she looks.

14. **Don't Argue Mentally**—when you are trying to understand the other person, it is a handicap to argue with him or her mentally as he or she is speaking. This sets up a barrier between you and the speaker.

15. **Use the Difference in Rate**—you can listen faster than the person talks, so use this rate difference to your advantage by trying to stay on the right track, anticipate what he or she is going to say, think back over what he or she has said, evaluate his or her development, etc. Speech rate is about 100 to 150 words per minute; thinking is 250 to 500.

16. **Listen for What Is Not Said**—sometimes you can learn just as much by determining what the other person leaves out or avoids when he or she speaks as you can by listening to what he or she says.

17. **Listen to How Something Is Said**—we frequently concentrate so hard on what is said that we miss the importance of the

emotional reactions and attitudes attached. A person's attitudes and emotional reactions may be more important than the words he or she says.

18. **Don't Antagonize the Speaker**—you may cause the other person to conceal his or her ideas, emotions, and attitudes by antagonizing him or her in any of a number of ways: arguing, criticizing, taking notes, not taking notes, asking questions, not asking questions, etc. Try to judge and be aware of the effect you are having on the other person. Adapt to him or her.

19. **Listen for the Person's Personality**—one of the best ways of finding out information about a person is to listen to him or her talk; as the person talks, you can begin to find out what his or her value system is, what he or she thinks about everything and anything, what makes the person tick.

20. **Avoid Jumping to Assumptions**—they can get you into trouble when trying to understand other persons. Don't assume that the person uses words in the same way you do; that the person didn't say what he or she meant but you understand what he or she meant; that person is avoiding looking you in the eye because he or she is telling a lie; that the person is trying to embarrass you by looking you in the eye; that he or she is distorting the truth because what he or she says doesn't agree with what you think; that the person is unethical because he or she is trying to win you over to his or her point of view; or that the person is angry because he or she is enthusiastic in presenting his or her views. Assumptions like these may turn out to be true, but often they just get in the way of your understanding and reaching an agreement of compromise.

21. **Avoid Classifying the Speaker**—it has some value, but beware! Too frequently we classify someone as one type of person and then try to fit everything he or she says into what makes sense coming from that type of person. People are unpredictable and won't necessarily fit into your classifications.

22. **Avoid Hasty Judgment**—wait until all the facts are in before making any judgments.

23. **Recognize Your Own Prejudice**—try to be aware of your own feelings toward the speaker, the subject, the occasion and allow for these prejudgments.

24. **Identify Type of Reasoning**—frequently it is difficult to sort out good and faulty reasoning, but it is so important that a listener make every effort to spot faulty reasoning when he or she hears it.

25. **Evaluate Facts and Evidence**—as you listen, try to identify not only the significance of the facts and evidence but also their relatedness to the argument.

Strategies for Intervention

1. Listen actively
2. Encourage the open expression of feelings
3. Help the person gain an understanding of the crisis
4. Help the individual gradually accept reality
5. Help the person explore new ways of coping with problems
6. Link the person to a social network

The caregiver must also be aware of what Clinebell describes as nonconstructive response to crises that persons are engaged in at the moment. There are eight such responses to crises that lead into emotional blind alleys and increase vulnerability to future and personality illness:

1. Denial that a problem exists
2. Evasion of the problem (via alcohol, for example)
3. Refusal to seek or accept help
4. Inability to express or master negative feelings
5. Failure to explore the nature of the crisis
6. Failure to explore alternative solutions

7. Projection onto others of total responsibility for causing and/or curing the crisis
8. Turning away from friends and family

The counselor should be alert to the presence of these malignant responses in order to help the person move away from them and toward the following healthy ways of coping:

1. Facing the problem
2. Enlarging one's understanding of it
3. Expressing and working through negative feelings such as resentment, anxiety, and guilt
4. Accepting responsibility for coping with the problem
5. Exploring alternative ways of handling it
6. Separating the changeable from the unchangeable in the situation
7. Accepting the unchangeable as unchangeable
8. Surrendering grandiose, burdensome aspects of one's self-image
9. Opening channels of communication with other helping persons among relatives, friends, and professional persons
10. Taking steps, however small, to handle the problem constructively

Helping Strategies for Crisis Intervention

1. **Establish the Relationship:**
    - Convey involvement, acceptance
    - Reinforce help-seeking
    - Invite to work
    - Provide structure

2. **Define the Problem:**
    - Define in client's terms
    - Explore depth, implications, changeability of concern
    - Be specific and allow open-ended exploration
    - Focus on "now and how" versus "then and why," (help prioritize)

- Check out final definition with client
- Make mutual, explicit contract based on realistic expectations for both

3. **Explore Feelings:**
   - Acknowledge
   - Accept
   - Explore implications of feelings
   - Why explore them
   - When not to deal with them
   - Promote hope
   - Reduce anxiety
   - Reduce denial, blame

4. **Explore Past Coping Attempts:**
   - Transition from problem to problem-solving
   - Take inventory of client's style and internal and external resources
   - Avoid solutions tried or reexplore prematurely rejected solutions

5. **Explore Alternatives and Develop Action Plan:**
   - Generate alternatives collaboratively, if possible
   - Explore consequences
   - Explore how client feels about alternative

Guidelines for Making Referrals

These guidelines are intended to facilitate the process of determining those needs that cannot be met by the pastoral care ministry. For example, a person may come for help, and it is determined he or she should be referred to Alcoholics Anonymous or some other agency. All referrals are made in consultation with the pastor and extreme care will be exercised to ensure proper processing of such needs.

1. **Define the Problem**
   The first step in the referral process is to clarify the person's particular problem or need. Failure to arrive at an accurate assessment of the person's problem can lead to a feeling of rejection and even distrust. Before suggesting that a person with alcoholism go to AA, it is important to find out how he or she sees the problem. If matters are not clear, then this is the point to ask questions. The statement may go something like this: "I want to make sure that I am giving you the most helpful information. Can you tell me a little about the basis of your request?"

2. **Prepare Person for Referral**
   Mention the possibility of referral early in any relationship in which help is likely to occur. This will prepare the person for the referral in the event one needs to be made.

3. **Encourage Person to Engage in Process**
   The person should take responsibility for making his or her own appointment should a referral be necessary. It is important that a person have the feeling that he or she is participating in finding the best possible solution of his or her problem.

How to Refer

Once the request is clear, the caregiver consults with the pastor, who provides advice regarding referral.

1. If possible, give the person a name of an individual, e.g., a secretary, when referring to an agency.

2. Although it may be helpful to refer a person to a specific person, this is not always possible. Familiarity with the personnel and the function of each agency will help you explain. A 3x5 index card file has been created with names of agencies and persons who are responsible for a particular resource.

Potential Problems with Referrals

Even when referrals are handled appropriately, the possibility of problems are present. The caregiver should be aware of them.

1. **Rejection**
   The client may interpret the suggestion of referral elsewhere as a rejection by the helper. The client might feel unaccepted and pushed away. He or she might increase efforts to please the helper and regain interest; he or she might react with anger and reject the idea; or he or she might not follow through on the referral and feel less inclined to approach the helper again.

2. **Guilt**
   The client may interpret a referral as the result of the feelings he or she has exposed in talking with a helper, such as anger, aggressiveness, or sexual acting out, which the client feels guilty about. Referral would then have a special meaning to the person. If the person is concerned by his or her own problems, he or she might feel he or she has also upset the helper, who out of anxiety, recommends that the person seek professional help as a control of impulse or to cleanse him or her. The client may feel his or her trust was misplaced in the helper or regret opening up. If the person follows through on a referral at all, he or she would then be less inclined to expose him- or herself at all.

3. **Anxiety**
   A client (appropriately) would have some fear about being referred to a strange person or unfamiliar setting. It is usually helpful to provide the person with a name and a telephone number and alert the referral resource that the client has been referred and the reasons for this action.

4. **Special Fears**
   The client may have special fears related to referral to a psychiatric service or psychological agency. Such a referral

may mean to the person that he or she is considered in need of hospitalization, special control, or is mentally unbalanced. Referral to an employment service may suggest that the person should work, which may remind him or her of a previous traumatic experience in looking for work. Referral for public assistance may also reinforce the person's fears about investigation or helplessness and inadequacy. With all referrals of minors, parental involvement is necessary, which could involve all kinds of unique problems and fears.

5. **Separation**
   Fear should not be minimized as it relates to the separation from the helper. This can be present even after a relatively short relationship, but particularly after a period of time during which the client has obviously formed a relationship with the helper.

The Family Trap

The Family Trap is an educational tool used in drug and alcohol education to give clear and accurate information about substance abuse. The film highlights the effects of chemical dependence on the family, clearly pointing out how it effects each personality type, i.e., the hero child who becomes a superachiever in an attempt to bring self-worth to the family as a result of the lack of emotional stability in the family. Or the scapegoat who is usually a low achiever who acts out looking for approval outside the family (to the pseudofamily) but getting no attention at all. Scapegoats are high suicide risk persons. The film shows how the environment of a family struggling with drug or alcohol problems causes members, especially the children, to develop coping skills to adapt to the situation.

Effects of Alcoholism of the Family

Attempts to deny problem	Denial of alcoholism in family
	Denial of problems in family unit
	Feelings of embarrassment, shame over drinking episodes
	Hopes rise, then fall; confused feelings
Attempts to eliminate problem	Isolate, pulling away from others
	Loss of perspective
	Alcoholic becomes focal point of family
	Family tries to control drinking episodes
	Loss of self-esteem, anger, resentment begins to escalate
	Family becomes obsessed with the alcoholic
	Sober adult begins to depend more on the children for emotional support
Reorganization	Tension erodes family structure
	Periods of hopefulness, periods of numbness
	Communication breaks down
	Compulsive behavior starts
	Fear of insanity
	Violence occurs
	Money problems
	Continued loss of self-esteem and self-worth
Attempts to reorganize despite problem	Crisis occurs
	Family members begin to be crisis oriented
	Sober adult becomes manager, decision maker
	Activities increase; family member may become a do-aholic
	Increased loss of self-esteem
Attempts to escape relationship	Terminal stage of relationship
	Separation, divorce

	Recovery of whole family unit
	Reorganization of part of family

Alcoholism is a family disease. It is a threefold disease—physical, emotional, and spiritual. The family member catches the emotional and spiritual parts. Some of the typical symptoms seen in many family members follow below:

Anger	Inconsistency
Rage, resentment	Super responsibility
Workaholism	Fear of unknown
Confusion	Hopelessness
Low self-esteem	Sexual problems
Verbal abusiveness	Personality changes
Mood swings	Sensitivity to criticism
unhappiness	Fear
Lying	Changing activities
Denial	Anxiety
Sleeping problems	Seriousness
Perfectionism	Feelings of inadequacy
Jealousy	Feelings of superiority
Appearance suffers	Tension
Jumpiness	Defensiveness
Secretiveness	Demanding behavior
Trapped/hostage feeling	Drug use
Erratic behavior	Family problems
Fear of insanity	Controlling behavior
Alcohol use/abuse	Compulsive behavior
Inability to function	Hypochondria
Fear of failure	Escapism
Intolerance	Peace at any price

Rescuing behavior	Suicidal thoughts
emotional yo-yo	Numbness
Loss of personal identity	Leaving it up to God
Self-pity	No talk rules
Physical abusiveness	People pleasing
Enabling	Loss of communication
Memory problems	Intellectualization
Intimidation	Repression of feelings
Loss of friends	Emotional withdrawal
Distortion of reality	Inability to make decisions
Resignation, giving up	Inability to trust decisions

All these symptoms are tractable by attending the breakthrough concept family program and Al-Anon family groups.

Chapter 8
Navigating Pastoral Pitfalls

Now that a successful program of pastoral care for crisis intervention has been implemented, there are yet some timeless rules of the road to observe. These rules, if followed, will keep you on track so you can make your journey successful. Remember you are now joined together, pastor and people, "caring enough to share," joined for better or for worse. Prayerfully it is for better. Unfortunately, the honeymoon is sometimes short-lived and the blissful moments soon come to an end. While you have made progress, at times you might encounter unnoticeable pits prepared as traps. Consequently, we will need some travel tips to make it to the journey's end.

First, a matter of top priority is the issue of sexual harassment and misconduct. This trap can and will destroy your entire ministry. Identifying this trap is of paramount importance. Trying to conceal and cover it up will only make it worse. A helpful hint for self-preservation is not allowing yourself to be caught alone with members of the opposite sex. This is important because of the magnitude of sexual harassment cases that have become widespread in recent years. Follow the scripture, "Wise as a serpent but harmless as a dove" (Matthew 10:16 KJV). We must be very clear on what is the basis of harassment. There is an article by Manis Friedman that defines harassment in plain and simple terms. He writes:

> Harassment indicates a lack of understanding of and respect for human sexuality. We can't turn it on or off whenever we wish. It's always there just under the

> surface. And when someone comes and tries to force it to the forefront of our beings, when we don't want it, or are not ready—that's harassment. You have to respect the space that others create around themselves. Morality says: when you see a weakness in someone, don't take advantage of it. Respect it, go around it, don't disturb it; don't enter where you are not invited.[20]

When we understand this, I believe it makes us all better people.

Another pitfall that challenges a pastor's leadership is the issue associated with change. One should begin with the fact that change is not easy, and there is a risk factor involved in the process. Navigating change should be of paramount importance. To begin with, one should be able to identify whether or not a particular congregation is prone to resisting change or if it readily accepts it. There is specific evidence that informs one of the readiness to move forward in the initiation of change or if there are indications suggesting to forego the intended change. In his book *Strategies for Change*, Lyle E. Shaller makes key observations on how to identify characteristics that are favorable to change and those that are unfavorable:

> The supportive environment for change shares several characteristics with the complacent organization but the differences are more significant than the similarities. The number one difference if it exists, is on a plateau in size while the most hospitable environments are found in numerically growing movements and organizations.[21]

In other words, if the change is being introduced and it's in a growing congregation, more than likely it will be accepted. However, if it is in an apathetic or complacent one, it will be impossible to succeed.

The important thing to recognize is if you are in a situation where change is to be made and the movement or organization is complacent and resistant to change, it will be necessary to work on what I call a systems overhaul. There are eight components to getting things in order to minimize the resistance:

1. Enhance pastoral care, not necessarily targeting those who have problems, but those who just want to be heard. This is an opportune time to doing one-on-one meetings. That will give you an idea what members are thinking spiritually and otherwise. You will also discover what it is that's driving the congregation.
2. Initiate a program of visitation by various groups who are happy about participating in the process of enhancing the relationships.
3. Take a look at the historical background. Identify those strands of local tradition that can be affirmed and built upon in building for the future.
4. Introduce the formation of ad hoc committees that focus on challenging the status quo and planning for a tomorrow that they believe will be different from yesterday.
5. Identify and respect influential volunteers who give support to new ideas.
6. Led by the pastor, identify and celebrate the victories, however minor they may be.
7. Create a reliable and accurate system of internal communication.
8. Avoid surprising people.

There are other traps that you need to be aware of. A pastor in a stressed out or burned out condition will not attract people in droves to his or her church. It's been demonstrated by research that newcomers want to get a fix on the clergyperson early on. They want to know whether or not the pastor is a good enough authority. Is he or she trustworthy? Does he or she have a quality of being? Does he or she express a sense of caring that feels authentic? Newcomers size up the pastor more by what he or she communicates nonverbally than by what is said. Even if newcomers are attracted to a congregation for other reasons, they won't join unless they felt good about the pastor.

What are you communicating to your congregation right now? Overwhelming tiredness, or a sense of being grateful to be alive and to be in ministry with God's people? If your energy level is low, getting the words just right won't make a difference. If you're upset or distraught, working harder and smiling stiffly won't fool anybody. No wonder many clergy have a recurring dream (or nightmare) of leading Sunday morning worship while stark naked. The old hymnbook just isn't big enough to hide behind.

One of the leading topics that fills the headlines today is health care. We ought to be concerned with clergy health care. The only way we will be a healthy presence among our people is to keep ourselves healthy. That's where self-care comes in—doing all that is necessary to win out against the twin destroyers: stress and burnout.

What Happens When You Cross Your Stress Threshold?

Decrease in Perception

Under normal circumstances we can take in from our environment all the data we need to function well. Under prolonged stress, the amount of data we can process diminishes. Most of us know the effects of those extra full days: services Sunday morning and then attending a church event all afternoon and another engagement in the evening. By Sunday evening we realize we are only hearing a fraction of the conversations being directed our way. It's like overloading a computer. The screen flashes, "Data Overload Error—Cannot Save This Page."

Perceived Loss of Options

When we cross our stress threshold, we cannot see clearly all the options available to us (like the disciples after the crucifixion—all they could think about was to go and lock themselves up). At times like these, our friends can be very helpful and important to us because they can often see alterities that we cannot. The ability to see options is one of the most valuable things we can offer parishioners when tragedy strikes their lives.

Regression to Infantile Behavior

When we're stressed, we tend to revert to old, familiar behavior patterns. It's important to remember how we reacted to stress as a child and identify those behaviors that, if acted out while in the role of clergyperson, would jeopardize our credibility.

Inability to Make Changes in Destructive Relationship Patterns

When our lives are in stress, we may find it difficult to extricate ourselves from relationships that are toxic to us. I am much less able to confront someone when I'm under excessive stress because that would mean making changes, and I simply can't introduce more stress to my life. When people make unreasonable demands on me, I find it easier to say yes than to hold my ground. I take on more work because I simply don't have the emotional energy to say no.

Fatigue

When we are under excessive stress, we need more rest and sleep than usual. In clergy transition seminars, clergypersons are encouraged to give themselves permission to rest more while they make their move into new jobs and roles. The confusion and self-doubt that occur in times of stress are often debilitating. We wonder if we are losing our capacity to cope or are simply getting too old.

When a person remains in a stressful situation over an extended period, he or she burns out. Stress and burnout are quite different in their manifestation. With stress, too much change or novelty forces people to overuse their adjustment capacities, and after a period of time they become either physically or emotionally ill. Burnout, on the other hand, can occur when people overuse their listening or caring capacities. They become consumed by too many needy people or too much responsibility over long periods of time. If not carefully monitored, pastors can very easily succumb to this pitfall. Be on the lookout for the following:

- **Decreased energy**—physically, the individual has difficulty keeping up the pace.
- **Decreased self-esteem**—the individual feels a sense of personal failure related to work or vocation.

- **Output exceeding input**—the person has poured more and more of him- or herself into a job or project, and the expected payoff or rewards are not forthcoming.
- **Sense of helplessness, hopelessness, being trapped**—the individual is unable to perceive alternate ways of functioning.
- **Cynicism and negativism**—the individual is down on self, others, the job, institutions, etc.

Burnout affects us at four levels:

1. Biologically, specific physical symptoms appear.
2. Psychologically, our emotional makeup is measurably altered.
3. Sociologically, a dysfunctional relationship exists between ourselves and our work, and possibly between our family and our church as well.
4. Spiritually, our worldview or view of reality is significantly altered.

Should you by chance end up in the trap of stress and burnout, keep in mind the following: When flux, change, and transition make us sick unto death, the bedrock of spiritual practices can serve as a sure support as well as reading the psalms, singing old familiar hymns, and being cared for by the people of our church. Remember, no matter how bad things get, never give up on hope. To have a vibrant parish ministry, we need the strong base provided by good primary relationships, spiritual nurture, and adequate rest. Unfortunately, parish ministry is so demanding that it can easily preempt other aspects of our lives. Most married clergy have experienced tension between family responsibilities and parish demands. Single clergy may not experience as many demands from significant people in their lives, but they are just as vulnerable to the consuming nature of parish ministry.

Spiritual disciplines can be for us the regular path by which we open ourselves to the grace of God. They can become the process by which we allow our own emptiness, our lack of perspective. Taking a sabbatical is also another strategy that you might want to embrace. There are grants available to churches that are enrolled in a program sponsored by the Lily Foundation.

Finally, there is a bit of advice that will help in navigating the pitfalls that have been noted above. It is a warning that comes from my military experience while going through basic training. There were explosives hidden below the surface of the ground. These explosives were designed to be detonated by pressure from a vehicle or a person. We were taught to look out for the land mines. Ministry has its land mines that must be avoided if we are to make the journey successful.

There will be times when your belief and trust in Jesus is down to a flickering flame and you consider walking away from your source of peace, hope, and joy. But remember no matter how loud the negative internal dialogue gets, it does not speak the truth. It is in the dark moments that negative internal dialogue likes to remind you of your weaknesses, limitations, broken dreams, and desires yet to be fulfilled. It hits hard and hurts deeply. It feels like you are hanging on to the side of a cliff by your fingertips with raging waters beneath you. Know that Jesus is there kneeling over the cliff and reaching out His hand, saying, "Let me help you."

There is a prayer that I often recite while doing in my daily devotions that you should remember:

> When evil darkens our world, give us light
> When despair numbs our souls, give us hope.
> When we stumble and fall lift us up.
> When doubts assail us, give us faith.
> When nothing seems sure, give us trust.
> When ideals fade, give us vision.
> When we lose our way, be our guide.
> That we may find serenity in your presence and purpose
> in doing your will.

How do we integrate our personal and professional life in such a way that transforms crisis into opportunities and moves us in the direction of lessening our stress?

During the tenure of my pastoral role, I have discovered that how I function in the pastoral context is, to a large degree, determined by my positive expectation of the future, which involves being combat ready.

This requires going into battle having on the whole armor. The apostle Paul in Ephesians reminds us to put on the whole armor of God, that we may be able to stand against the wiles of the devil (Ephesians 6:11).

Make certain that you do not place yourself, your family, and your congregation on a cliff, thereby creating a breach that will come back to haunt you. Remember none of us are perfect. Take extra precautions to recognize the need to repair whatever breach that might be present either by your mistake or the congregation's. When correcting members, do it quietly and make a point of complimenting the individual. For example, you might say, "You did well in handling the dispute, but you seemed to have prejudged without considering all the facts."

Don't try to save the whole world. Follow the scriptures. Never minimize the political or economic oppression, cruelty, domestic abuse, and simple bullying that is so rampant in our world today.

My child, right now you may have people that are with you, but you need the right kind of people—praying people, godly people. In order for anything to succeed, you have to have the right people at the right time. It's nothing like doing the right thing at the wrong time. One of the greatest things that can block progress is distractions. Everyone robed and collared isn't anointed: be aware of the folk who have a church face and an everyday face. Listen, we know there are no perfect people, but we've got to get over the things in our past. This is your season … Don't sit and complain about how nobody will help you; get up and help yourself. The things you've been through will help shape your ministry. It'll help you put your ministry in the proper perspective. You have to reframe what has happened to you and let it help what will happen to you. Don't use it as an excuse but as a crutch to get you to where you're going. In summary, I leave with you five keys to building trust:

1. Express feelings, not just thoughts.
2. Listen to verbal and nonverbal communication and respond to both.
3. When something goes wrong, ask what, not who.
4. Offer encouragement instead of criticism.
5. Follow through on commitments.

Chapter 9
Cruising into the Twilight of Retirement

Webster's Dictionary defines cruise control as an electronic device in a vehicle that controls the throttle so as to maintain constant speed. It also controls the amount of fuel consumption while the device is in action. Likewise, the minister nearing the finish line of ministry should be in the position of doing so in a cruise control.

By now things like life insurance and medical benefits should already be in place. One should never accept an assignment without having an eye on the future. This means that as you begin, know that it is not for an eternity. It is for a season, and there will come a time for that season to end. For some it will be a brief season, for others it will be a long haul. Whether its long or short, we must look for the road signs posted along the way to lead to the finish line. While it still may seem far off in the distance, every now and then you ought to view the future. Every effort should be made to ensure you have enough energy to make it to the goal.

In the words of Bob Kaylor:

> Having spiritual stamina and running with a purpose. Making sure you are surrounded by wise mentors and a marvelous team of lay leaders if you are going to make to the finish line.[22]

As you go, never get so busy that you are not able to take time out for the necessary medical checkups at least every six months. For some this schedule may vary depending on your general health. Make certain that you include some form of recreation such as football, baseball, golf, or other sports activity. This is where you can establish wonderful friendships and relationships. I recall being introduced to racquetball by the chairman of the diaconate ministry (deacon Marvin Moore). We had weekly matches, and this was the beginning of a long-lasting friendship that exists even to this date. It not only enhanced our friendship, but my physical health as well.

As you get closer to the finish line, make sure that you are not carrying unnecessary baggage that's distracting you while helping a stranded member in the congregation.

These are practical guidelines that will activate your spiritual cruise control as you head to the finish line of the journey. Another important point is don't be afraid to teach your people the importance of caring for their under shepherd. I made certain that my congregation was aware that Wednesday was my family day. This was time carved out of the schedule for a date with my wife and family. Also be sure ask your employer to have a plan in place to provide for your continuing education. This will include expenses for attending conferences, workshops, and so on.

Be careful not to allow wolves dressed in sheep's clothing to break in and attack innocent sheep. Arm yourself with a pastoral care and counseling network. Most important, feed your conversation a wholesome diet of the Word. Make certain you pray up, rest up, read up, study up, love up, mount up, and look up.

Make sure you carry these seven ups in your spiritual backpack:

1. Pray up: Therefore, confess your sins to each other and Pray for each other so that you may be healed. The Prayer of a righteous person is powerful and effective (James 5:16 NIV).

2. Rest up: Ministry can sometimes be exhausting we need time to rest up. And he said, My presence shall go with thee, and I will give thee rest (Exodus 33:14 KJV).

3. Read up: And when this epistle is read among you, cause that it be read also in the church of the Laodiceans; and that ye likewise read the epistle from Laodicea (Colossians 4:16 KJV).

4. Study up: Study to shew thyself approved unto God, a workman that needeth not to be ashamed, rightly dividing the word of truth (2 Timothy 2:15 KJV).

5. Love up: And now these three remain: faith, hope and love. But the greatest of these is love' (1 Corinthians 13:13 NIV).

6. Mount up: But they that wait upon the Lord shall renew their strength; they shall mount up with wings as eagles; they shall run, and not be weary; and they shall walk and not faint (Isaiah 40:31 KJV).

7. Look up: And when these things begin to come to pass, Then look up, and lift your heads; for your redemption draweth nigh (Luke 21:28 KJV).

Having these seven ups will provide extra nourishment and refreshment as you near the finish line and hear these words, "Well done, thy good and faithful servant; thou hath been faithful over a few things, I will make you ruler over many things: enter thou into the joy of thy Lord" (Matthew 25:23 KJV).

Epilogue

I return to the bridge builder illustration cited earlier in the book. It is interesting that in recent months we have heard a lot of hype about building walls instead of building bridges. I am somewhat annoyed at that in a time that crisis seem to be the order of the day. And yet more focus seems to be on building walls. When I think about walls, I see separation, isolation, discrimination, alienation, and incarceration.

What we need are bridges that lead to liberation, bridges that brings people together. One thing that describes my work in the ministry is bridge builder.

While serving as president of the Association of Brooklyn Clergy for Community Development for over twenty years, we were building bridges to community revitalization by developing over 250 units of low-income housing. Ruth and I were building bridges while taking in young people whom I had never met before and assisting in housing them and helping them through school. We were building bridges when interceding on behalf of community residents amid opposition to single residence occupancy for persons who were HIV positive.

The journey has been long and hard, but I am grateful that it has had been blessed along the way. Special advice to those who come after me. Those who are committed to making life just a little better because you passed this way. Enjoy the trip but pay attention to the spiritual road signs posted along the way:

> "Peace I leave with you, my peace I give unto you: not as the world giveth, give I unto you. Let not your heart be troubled, neither let it be afraid" (John 14:27 KJV).

"Not by might nor by power, but by my Spirit, saith the Lord of hosts" (Zechariah 4:6b KJV).

"For I know the plans I have for you, declares the Lord, plans to prosper you and not to harm you, plans to give you hope and a future" (Jeremiah 29:11 NIV).

"To him who is able to keep you from stumbling and to present you before his glorious presence without fault and great joy" (Jude 1:24 NIV).

"And surely I am with you always, even to the very end of the age" (Matthew 28:20b NIV).

"Wherefore God also hath highly exalted him and given him a name which is above every name" (Philippians 2:9 KJV).

"Fret not thyself because of evildoers, neither be thou envious against the workers of iniquity" (Psalm 37:1 KJV).

"No weapon that is formed against thee shall prosper; and every tongue that shall rise against thee in judgment thou shalt condemn" (Isaiah 54:17 KJV).

"Ye are of God, little children, and have overcome them: because greater is he that is in you, than he that is in the world" (1 John 4:4 KJV).

"For God so loved the world, that he gave his only begotten Son, that whosoever believeth in him should not perish, but have everlasting life" (John 3:16 KJV).

"But he was wounded for our transgressions, he was bruised for our iniquities: the chastisement of our peace

> was upon him; and with his stripes we are healed" (Isaiah 53:5 KJV).

One final note is that the process and skills that have been sketched here are not by any means developed in a few weeks or a few months. The birth and growth of a first-rate caregivers' ministry takes several years. It has been said that the journey of a thousand miles begins with the first step. The significance of this journey is highlighted by Oden:

> When the soul sets out from the Egypt of this life to go to the promised land, it necessarily goes by certain stages. The stages are those by which the soul journeys from earth to heaven. The history of the soul is like a journey that has a promised, but as yet not experienced conclusion. While in the midst of the journey we may not yet see how the road could possible wind toward a fitting conclusion, so evidently does it seem to be going contrary ways. The function of the soul guide (caregiver) is to help interpret, insofar as possible, the whole journey. This interpretation is better made by observing carefully the path already taken, both by humanity and the individuals, by accurately reading the present situation, and by providing hope and encouragement that the final destination will provide a full understanding of the prevailing absurdities of the present and past.[23]

Being with persons and for persons during their struggles along the road demonstrates that we are all working together with God to help individuals make it to the final destination.

Appendix
Sermons

Help for the Journey

Anchor I: It was God that bought Israel out (Exodus 13:3,9,14,16).

One of the things that Israel (God's people) never fully grasped was that it was God that brought them out of Egypt. Moses was only instrumental.

Read Exodus 14:11–12.

Well, God came through for Israel and all were blessed! They even sang songs to the Lord and danced (block party?)

Anchor II: God was leading Israel every step of the way.

Another one of Israel's mistakes was not realizing that it was not only God that brought them out, but that it was God that was leading them.

Read Exodus 13:17–18.

God led His people to a seemingly dead end! Sea in front, mountains on the right and left. And Pharaoh's army approaching from the rear!

The Wilderness is God's Gym

The wilderness is where most of God's people get stuck!

Many of God's people today share the same fate of ancient Israel. They are delivered out of Egypt but never enter into the victorious Christian life (which Canaan was a type).

Question: Why is this?

Answer: Many of God's people don't understand the purpose of the wilderness.

This is found in Deuteronomy 8:1–4:

1. True humility, verse 2 (If my people would humble themselves)
2. Revelation of self, verse 2 (Isaiah 6:1, "woe is me")
3. Test your obedience

In the wilderness you learn to be dependent on God and how to trust Him.

- Food
- Water
- Guidance

Contributed by my only son, Keith Leroy Whitney. He prepared this outline for Bible study but passed away before he was able to present the lesson. Born in 1964, died in 2001. May he rest in peace.

The Right Place, the Wrong Time

Text: John 5:1-9

There is a possibility that we can be at the right place and yet our timing can be so overshadowed by a multitude of activities and loyalties that we miss the purpose for which we long for and desire to accomplish in our lives.

The right place is hard to define in our world today, and many of our young people are trying desperately to find the right place. There must be a place in life where I can escape half thoughts, half-hearted devotion, half resolutions, distractions, and indecisiveness. There must be someplace where we can get it all together.

There is a need for this trend of thought, because life in this period bears a mute testimony to the fact that we are somewhat confused, misled, and we have misinterpreted many significant happenings within our lifetime.

There is a great difference between a good individual and a devoted individual. A good individual keeps the commandments of God, but he or she lacks fervor, great loyalty, and great convictions. But he or she is devoted who not only observes the commandments but does so willingly, promptly, and with a good heart, even when no one is watching.

There is human madness in our day, and it is rocking the world far out of hand. Sociology, technology is baffled and bewildered. This madness is reflected in all areas of human life. It appears at times that this madness is reflected in all areas of human life. It appears at times that the universe is irritated by the reckless behavior of the creatures who dwell here. Floods, earthquakes, tornadoes, fires, explosions, disaster, and other happenings in the world seem to signal the displeasure of heaven at our recklessness.

An evil spirit is rampant in industry, labor, government, educational circles, home life, crime, drug traffic, racism, and in all areas of our involvement. Maniacs have been exalted to positions of power and prestige in many areas of our society. Mad persons seem to be enthroned at crucial levels in our troubled world—people who cannot be bound by conscience or concern for other human beings. We are bruised, bleeding, and dying, and those who tell us they can help us are usually in the right places but their timing is confused.

During all our confusion, we are afraid of one another. We can't seem to learn to trust one another. Somehow, we must again learn to be captivated by ideas and involved in making our world safe for those who wait at the pool of mercy for the blessing.

For we, like Israel of old, have drifted too far from the God whom we claim when we say in God we trust. Even our Watergate scandal and other recent political scandals are signs of a society sliding down the slippery slopes of degradation. In times when we can't trust the one who holds the highest office in the nation, who can be trusted?

The message of our time seems to be that we are in the right place; our message reminds us that we are in the right place. When we view society, there are two important messages, and they seemingly come from opposing forces. Society says the youth are wild. Lock them up. The church says restore them to a useful place. Society says condemn them. The church says heal their broken spirits. Society says they are hopeless. The church says they can be rehabilitated. Society says they are wasted lives. The church says there is spark of divinity in them. They are gold and can be salvaged.

Verse 3 reads, "In these lay a great multitude of impotent folk, of blind, halt, withered, waiting for the moving of the water."

Jesus has the power to gather up fragmented and shattered pieces of humanity and put them together again. This is all the redemptive process. Satanic forces leave humanity crippled, wounded, shattered, and bleeding by the roadside of life. Jesus is constantly looking for cripples. It is the right time to preach an uncompromising gospel. It's the right time to tell a dying world that He can restore. It is the right time for youth to marshal its forces and march under salvation's banner. It is the right time for those who are on the church's roll to stand up and be counted. It is high time to quit making excuses, apologies, and telling lies to cover up our shortcomings. It is high time to realize that the salvation of the world is at stake. It is the right time to speak up about what we know about this gracious God who has made a way out of no way. It is the right time to sing until the power of the Lord come down.

Unfortunately, we are in the wrong places. If we have problems at the local church, we can't help to straighten them out if we are at the wrong place. You can't make the choir better by sitting at home. Your intention may be good, but you are in the wrong place. You can't make the church stronger by calling everybody and talking about its weaknesses. You can't help others into the pool of salvation if you are not there when they are ready to go in.

The text tells us very vividly that Jesus had left Galilee and returned to Jerusalem in time for a feast, and immediately He went up to Jerusalem. As He passed the sheep market gate, there was a scene of broken bodies and diseased individuals that greeted Him. Nearby at a pool called Bethesda, He encountered a man who was serious about his faith and his hope for deliverance from his plight. Jesus has a record of picking one out of a crowd for special attention. It was reported that at a certain season an angel came down and troubled the water, and whoever was first in the water would be healed. But this man had been there for thirty-eight years.

He blamed his plight on the fact that there was no one who cared enough to see that he was first in so that he might be healed. The word

Bethesda means "The House of Mercy." Therefore, we can see that he was thirty-eight years at the house of mercy waiting for a blessing, and he could only blame his plight on the absence of another who was responsible for seeing that he got in the water. Thirty-eight years is a long time to wait for a blessing at the house of mercy. Thirty-eight years waiting and watching; thirty-eight years of toils and tears; of failure and fears; of weariness and wishing; of shattered dreams and broken hopes; of back and forth to the house of mercy; of disillusionment and disappointments; of discouragement and despair. Thirty-eight years at the house of mercy, desiring, pleading, coaxing, beseeching someone to help him get a blessing. But thirty-eight years at the house of mercy is too long.. But tragically some of us can be caught in this trap. Our church becomes a burden. Our crosses get too heavy. Our physical health begins to wane. Our youthful dreams can disappear. And we can still warm a pew and not realize a blessing. Jesus is speaking to him. You are at the right place, but your timing has been bad. Do you want to get out of it? Do you want to be whole? Would you like to get it together? Listen to his reply: I do want to, but other people get in my way. You see, when I don't get the blessing, someone else steps in and takes my place. They never put my name on the program. Nobody seems to know that I am here. People are always in front of me. My neighbor, the lady in the next pew, the preacher, the deacon, the old folks, the young folks, the man I work for, the people I associate with. I am a victim of being in the right place at the wrong time.

Jesus speaks to him again: Why not be responsible for yourself? Why not show your desire for a better life by action? Why not use this scene as an example of concern? Why not become involved, and your cares will disappear. In your concern for a better life, don't worry about the others. Take some weight for your success on your own shoulders. Take up your own bed and walk. Quit talking so loudly and start to do some of the things you talk about. You can make it if you try.

And on the same day, after thirty-eight years, he got up and walked. This miracle brought much trouble for Jesus and His disciples, but it moves us into a perspective where we can see ourselves.

If we would change our world, we must take heed. If we would be better people, we must listen. If we are to serve this present age, the lesson is here. If we are to contribute, a note of interest is enclosed. If we are to have better homes, schools, colleges, and professions, then take heed. Let us quit hiding behind others. Quit blaming our plight on the presence or absence of anyone else.

Quit developing alibis. Quit trying to outtalk others. And finally, like Jesus, take up your own responsibility.

Take up your own bed of responsibility and walk with it.

Let us not be guilty of being in the right place, at the house of mercy, and be all wrong about our timing.

Making the Best of a Bad Situation

Text: 2 Kings 5:1

He Was a Mighty Man of Valor, but He Was a Leper

All human beings struggle with conflict and contradiction. Such a man was Naaman the Syrian. He was a mighty man of valor, a glorious warrior, a military genius, a recognized leader of men, but he was a leper.

The terrible curse of leprosy was a burden on his life. The conflicts and contradictions of our lives burden us as well. Good thoughts battle bad thoughts. We care, yet we can kill. We have affection and anger, humility and pride, faith and doubt. We seek to be patient but desire immediate gratification. We accept salvation but still wrestle with sin. For every good situation, it seems there is a bad situation.

Like Naaman the Syrian, we have the one great burden we must bear: A loving father, but°... A caring mother, but°... An effective executive, but°... A good teacher, but°... An excellent manager, but°.... A beautiful child, but°... A great preacher, but°... A loyal friend, but°... A hard worker, but°...

All of us have a disadvantage, a cause of suffering in our lives. A thorn in our side, a bad situation.

Some bad situations are out of our control. There are the social realities of oppression. People make life difficult for us. They don't like us because of race, color, creed, class, gender, ethnic background, lack of education, achievement, or just plain jealousy.

Some people dislike you because you remind them of someone else you don't even know. That's a bad situation.

In Egypt God led people out when they got to the formidable Red

Sea. God opened up a highway for them. When they found themselves without food or water, God took little ravens and transformed them into a butcher and baker and fed the children of Israel. When they were without water, He made a spring within a rock. When the Jews found themselves victims of vicious Haman's evil plot to exterminate them, He raised up a queen to save. We must tell ourselves, *I can make it; God is my helper.* There are no mountains we can't climb, no oceans we can't swim, no battles we can't win, and no problems we can't solve if our Lord wills it. The scripture reminds us "we are more than conquers through Him who loves us" (Romans 8:37 NIV).

Whatever else may happen in our lives, know the most important battle of all, the fight for the salvation of our souls, has already been won. Jesus gives us the victory if we give Him our faith.

We as a people need to learn to do something for ourselves, rather than always expecting someone else to do things for us. Help often means getting what you need instead of what you want.

As someone once said, if you feed someone a fish, they will always be hungry. If you teach someone to fish, they will always eat.

In the text, God sent the little maid of Israel to Naaman. She told him where to go for help. The maid was not too self-righteous and hung up on her own oppression to give advice to a master. Naaman was not too arrogant and hung up on his own lordship to accept advice from a slave. All of us have a leprosy that only God can heal. Everyone has a sin that only the Lord can wash away. Each human being has one burden that only our savior can lift.

Obedience and faith will give you good results in a bad situation. When you can't help yourself, when other can't help you, the Lord always can.

Do whatever God tells you, even when the answer seems to easy. Namaan felt there should have been more to his salvation. If he had been given a more complicated answer to his problem, he would have asked no questions. However, he still did what the Lord said do and was healed.

If you follow instructions God gives you in prayer, Bible study, worship, and discipleship, the same will happen for you

After all, did not our Lord and Savior Jesus Christ make the best of a bad situation? He lived in a world where He was at a disadvantage.

He was discriminated against before He was born. There was no room in the inn. Jesus was born in a manger. His father, Joseph, died while Jesus was a teenager. Being the eldest son, He had to work as a carpenter to help out the family. Jesus was a Jew from Galilee, the most backward area of the Israelite nation. He was despised by Jews in Jerusalem, slandered by enemies, looked down on by religious leadership because He had no formal theological education, and misunderstood by even His own disciples.

He was betrayed by friends, abandoned by followers, tortured by Roman soldiers, and crucified for a crime He didn't commit. He was indeed the victim of bad situations. But the Lord made the best of them for Himself and all who believe. He turned agonizing death into glorious resurrection. He turned the darkness of the grave into the light of eternal life. The cross, a symbol of shame and defeat for the world, became for the church of Jesus Christ, a symbol of victory and salvation. The victim became the victor, defeating sin, death, and the devil.

I know what you are thinking, that Jesus is the Son of God, which is true, but you too are sons and daughters of God if you believe in the Son of God.

Are you a great person, but°...? Do people make life difficult for you? Does some thorn in your side plague your every move? Is there some disadvantage you have that keeps you from fulfillment in life? Does a problem you suffer from keep you worried and depressed? Has something happened to shatter your dream? Your vision? Your spirit? Your faith? Are things out of your control, defeating you?

Let go and let God. Turn it over to Him and let the Lord fight your battles. Despite the leprosy in your life, the Lord can cure it. He will make you a mighty man or woman of valor. The Lord can and will always get the best out of a bad situation.

Uncrossable Rivers

Text: Joshua 3:1ff

Our journey to the Promised Land is always filled with crises. Unpredictable and unexpected acts pop us that block our progress to where God is leading us. Some of you may have come to testify that there are some rivers that are uncrossable in your life. Rivers that are impossible to deal with. Nevertheless, God specializes in helping us through things that are impossible. Joshua 3 begins with the children of Israel on the banks of the River Jordan. Behind them is the wilderness where they have wondered for forty years.

On the other side of the River Jordan is the land of Canaan, the Promised Land, the land that flows with milk and honey. The land that was promised and guaranteed by God years ago. Our text brings us to crisis reached in Israel's history very similar to the first great crisis, when they passed through the Red Sea. The questions that arrest our attention are: (1) What do you do when you have stood on tiptoe anticipation, waiting year after year for promises that were in arm's reach, when suddenly a serious problem popped up that prevents you from going where God is leading? (2) Who do you look to when faced with impossible situations, uncrossable rivers, or unbeatable foes? The people of faith are always in crisis. In fact, faith creates crisis. But hold on, God is getting ready to perform one of the greatest miracles in the history of Israel.

There are timely lessons for those believers who are faced with uncrossable rivers. The challenge they face is: Shall they commit themselves to go forward to struggle with the seven nations of Canaan who are more powerful than they, or shall they go back to where they were? The issue is compounded by the condition of Jordan at this time. This is flood season, and Jordan is overflowing. They were faced with another crisis of equal proportion. To cross Jordon would lead them to pursue a course of action condemned by ten out of twelve of the spies sent out forty years before to assess the situation. This was a crisis on which their national future hung. It needed crisis insight. How could they cross this river and claim what God had already promised them? Let them turn back and their enthusiasm would evaporate, their unity would break up. Their whole history hung in the balance. History is not made by doing nothing.

Let them go forward, and with a sufficient amount of faith, their movement forward would defy any force that would try to stop them.

The crossing of Jordan is one of the major events in all of the Bible. Egypt, Red Sea, wilderness, Jordan, and Canaan all show us that what

God did for the children of Israel in the Old Testament He can do in our lives today. This text has a lot to say about our Christian life. It has a lot to say about what you do on your job. How you conduct yourself in school. The way you lead and guide in your home and in your family. It helps us to navigate through turbulent waters of adversity.

We see the spiritual significance of crossing over Jordan. Have you had the experience the children of Israel had when you turned your back on the wilderness, set your face toward the land of Canaan, and crossed over Jordan? There is a very practical message in this text. It has to do with the rivers of difficulty. It deals with the uncrossable rivers in our lives.

Today you may be facing a river of doubt, and others may be facing a river of weakness. Some may be facing a river of fear, and they can't seem to get over it. They can't quite get the victory over this uncrossable river in their lives.

Joshua 3 points us to some important strategies for facing uncrossable rivers. We first of all take note of the preparation to go forward. Three days had ended and the mobilization was complete. Despite the preparation on the part of Israel, the Jordan posed a serious problem—it was flooded, impassable (Joshua 3:15). What were they to do? How could they get across the Jordan? Was their hope for the long-awaited inheritance to be crushed on the rocks of the Jordan? Unless they crossed over, they could not receive the inheritance.

The Jordan River represented an obstacle to the Promised Land. The Promised Land represented a new life for the people of God, a victorious life of conquest and triumph, of abundance and fruitfulness.

In this passage, five different instructions are given by Joshua, his officers, and God. Five different instructions challenging everyone to have faith and to trust God. By faith, God would provide the way to cross over the Jordan. By faith, God would show how to overcome the problem and obstacle of the Jordan. By faith, God would make sure His people would receive the promised inheritance, the victorious life of the Promised Land. (1) There were instructions from the officers to the people (Joshua 3:3–4). They instructed the people to follow the ark. Remember, the ark was a symbol of God's presence. The people were to move out and follow the ark into the riverbed. They were to believe and trust the power of God. All through the years of the Christian journey, putting the Lord in front has been an act that has produced abundance fruit. (2) There were the instructions of Joshua to the people (Joshua 3:5). Joshua ordered the people to sanctify, consecrate, and purify themselves. This meant that the people were to prepare their hearts before the Lord. They were to pray, confess, repent, rededicate, and recommit their lives to God. This was to be symbolized by the outward acts of bathing and changing clothes and also by abstaining from sexual relations so that they could devote their full attention to the Lord (Exodus 19:10, 14–15, 1 Corinthians 7:1–6). (3) There were instructions from Joshua to the priests (ministers) (Joshua 3:6). This was a challenge for the priests to be strong in faith, to believe enough to take up the ark and move out ahead of the people. They were to courageously lead the people into the swift, dangerous currents of the flooding river. (4) There were instructions from God to Joshua (Joshua 3:7–8). Joshua needed to learn that God was with him just as God had been with Moses. Through the miraculous event about to take place, Joshua would be exalted in the eyes of all the Israelites. The people would know that he was chosen by God and that he followed and trusted God. As a result of this miracle about to take place, the people would highly esteem Joshua and follow his leadership. (5) There were the instructions from Joshua to the people (Joshua 3:9–13). Joshua declared the Word of the Lord, the assurance of His promise. God would provide the way to cross over the surging, raging currents of the flooding Jordan. God would enable His people to conquer the problem and cross over to secure their inheritance. There are several insights that was encompassed in Joshua's instructions. He explained the purpose of God's miracle and gave the reasons why God was going to make a way to cross over the Jordan (Joshua 3:10). It would prove that God was the living God. As the living God, He is the only true God who can actually save and deliver His people through all the trials of life, even the terrible trial of death. Because He is the living God, He alone is to be worshipped and served by people. The miracle also would prove that God will always give the power to defeat the enemies of His people. God will work through His people, giving them His own power and enabling them to drive out all enemies of the Promised Land. Joshua declared the assurance of God: the ark of God's presence would lead the way through the raging currents of the Jordan River. The people in turn were to believe and trust His miraculous power. In fact, they were to demonstrate and prove their trust. This was done by making preparations to build a memorial to God's power after they had crossed over the Jordan. Joshua explained the miracle. As soon as the priests set foot in the Jordan, the waters of the river would be cut off upstream. The waters would actually be stopped and begin to pile up in a heap (Joshua 3:13).

The significance of the Jordan River is a picture of the problems and difficulties, the trials and temptation that confront us throughout life. Faith in God is the only way to conquer the obstacles of life. Faith in God is the only way to conquer fear, additions, weaknesses, death, obsessions, suffering, and discouragement. It is true that God loves and cares for us. He cares about every problem that confronts us, and He wants to strengthen us to overcome all problems. He wants to show us the way to triumph over the obstacles that stand in our way. Believing God, trusting God, having faith in God—this is the only way you can become a conqueror throughout life. Faith in God is the victory that overcomes the world with all of its obstacles. Be it known that "for whatsoever is born of God overcometh the world: and this is the victory that overcometh the world, even our faith. Who is he that overcometh the world but he that believeth that Jesus is the Son of God" (1 John 5:4–5).

As you face the contrary winds that don't seem to cease, remember the words of Douglas Miller, which helps us to move forward with hope:

> Though the storms keep on raging in my life,
> Sometimes it's hard to tell my nights from day.
> Still that hope that lies within is reassured
> as I keep my eyes upon the distant shore;
> I know He'll lead me safely to that
> blessed place He has prepared
>
> But if the storms don't cease,
> and if the wind keeps on blowing in my life°…[24]

Notes

1 James C. Fenhagen, *Mutual Ministry: New Vitality for the Local Church* (New York: Harper & Row Publishers, 1997), 83.

2 Ira Wilson. *Make Me a Blessing*. (Nashville: R. H. Boyd Publishers, 1977), 350.

3 Author is unknown. There is another version written by Will Allen Dromgoole with minor variations.

4 Joy W. Laughridge. "When Will These Things Happen?" *Lectionary Homiletics*, October–November 2010, 60.

5 Marshall Shelley. *Ministering to Problem People in Your Church: What to Do with Well-Intentioned Dragons* (Minneapolis: Bethany House Publishers, 1985), 153.

6 Albert J. Raboteau. *Slave Religion: The "Invisible Institution" in the Antebellum South* (New York: Oxford University Press), 4.

7 E. Franklin Frazier. *The Negro Church in America* (New York: Schocken Books, 1974), 13.

8 C. Eric Lincoln. *Race Religion and the Continuing American Dilemma* (New York: Wang Publishers), 72.

9 Joan Blundall. "As the Heartland Bleeds, Where Is the Church?" *Laity Exchange* (San Leandro: Vespers Service, Sept 1987), 1.

10 Patricia Benner. "Conserving and Preserving Caring Practices." *Laity Exchange* (San Leandro: Vespers Service, July 1987), 1.

11 Nelson Vos. "Your Local Congregation: Is It Salt and Leaven and Light in the World?" *Laity Exchange* (San Leandro: Vespers Service, September 1988).

12 Rodger K. Bufford & Robert E. Buckler. "Counseling in the Church: A Proposed Strategy for Ministering to Mental Health Needs in the Church." *Journal of Pastoral Care* 6 no. 2, p.25.

13 Hans Kung. *The Church* (Garden City: Doubleday/Image Books, 1976), 301.

14 Colossian 2:9.

15 Compton, Beulah R., and Burt Galaway. *Social Work Processes*, 4th ed. (Belmont: Wadsworth Publishing Company, 1989), 505.

16 Cited by Gerald Caplan from a keynote address to Conference of Department of Psychiatry, Rutgers Medical School, and New Jersey Mental Health Association on June 8, 1972 by John C. Cassel.

17 Ibid.

18 David Switzer. *The Minister as Crisis Counselor* (Nashville: Abingdon Press, 1974), 32. Cited from Bruce A. Baldwin, "A Paradigm for the Classification of Emotional Crises: Implications for Crisis Intervention." *American Journal of Orthopsychiatry* 48 (1978):538–51.

19 Lydia Rapoport. *The State of Crisis: "Some Theoretical Considerations in Crisis Intervention: Selected Readings*, ed. by Howard J. Parad (New York: Family Service Association of America, 1965), 25–26.

20 Rabbi Manis Friedman. " The Morality of Weakness: Defining Sexual Harassment." Chabad.org.

21 Lyle E. Schaller. *Strategies for Change* (Nashville: Abingdon Press, 1993), 43.

22 Bob Kaylor. "Seven Keys to Making Your Worst Pastoral Move." *Homiletics* 29, no. 3 (May–June 2017) p. 3.

23 Thomas Oden. *Crisis Ministries: Classical Pastoral Care* (New York: Crossroads, 1986), 57.

24 Douglas Miller. www. Songlyrics.com/Douglas miller/my-soul has been anchored-lyrics.

Bibliography

Clinebell, Howard J., Jr. *Basic Types of Pastoral Care and Counseling*. Nashville: Abingdon Press, 1984.

____*Mental Health Through Christian Community*. Nashville: Abingdon Press, 1965.

Compton, Burt, and Beulah R. Galaway. *Social Work Processes*, 4th ed. Belmont: Wadsworth Publishing Company, 1989.

Crabb, Lawrence J. *Effective Biblical Counseling: A Model for Helping Caring Christians Become Capable Counselors*. Grand Rapids: Zondervan Publishing House, 1971.

De Gruchy, John W. *Theology and Ministry in Context and Crisis: A South African Perspective*. Grand Rapids: William B. Eerdmans Publishing, 1986.

Erikson, Erik H. *Childhood and Society*. New York: W. W. Norton & Company, Inc., 1963.

Felton, Carroll M. *The Care of Souls in the Black Church*. New York: Martin Luther King Fellows Press, 1980.

Frazier, E. Franklin. *The Negro Church in America*. New York: Schocken Books, 1974.

Gerkin, Charles V. *Crisis Experience in Modern Life*. Nashville: Abingdon Press, 1979.

Golan Naomi. *Treatment in Crisis Situations*. New York: The Free Press, 1978.

Gottlieb, Benjamin. *Social Support Strategies: Guidelines for Mental Health Practice*. Beverly Hills: Sage Publications, 1983.

Grinder, John E., Bandler, Richard. *The Structure of Magic II: A Book about Communication and Change.* Palo Alto: Science and Behavior Books, 1976.

Guntrip, Harry. *Psychoanalytic Theory: Therapy and the Self.* New York: Basic Books Inc.,1973.

Hale, Janice. *Black Children.* Provo: Bringham Young University Press, 1982.

Hicks, H. Beecher, Jr. *Preaching Through a Storm.* Grand Rapids: Zondervan Publishing House, Ministry Resources Library, 1987.

Haugk, Kenneth C. *Christian Caregiving: A Way of Life.* Minneapolis: Augsburg Publishing House, 1984.

McRay, William J. *Christian Caregiving: A Way of Life Leader's Guide.* Minneapolis: Augsburg Publishing Company, 1986.

Hayes, Helen, Vander poel. *Health Care Ministry.* New York: Paulist Press, 1990.

Hepworth, Dean N., Larsen, JoAnn. *Direct Social work Practice: Theory and Skills.* Chicago: The Dorsey Press, 1986.

Hiltner, Seward. *Preface to Pastoral Theology.* Nashville: Abingdon Press, 1958.

Hulme, William E. *Pastoral Care & Counseling.* Minneapolis: Augsburg Publishing House, 1981.

Hurst, David. *The Shepherding of Black Christians.* Ann Arbor: University Microfilms, 1981.

Kung, Hans. *The Church.* Garden City: Doubleday/Image Books, 1976.

Lattimore, Vergel L. *Pastoral Care Strategies of Black Pastors.* Ann Arbor: University Microfilms, 1984.

Lincoln, C. Eric. *Race, Religion and the Continuing American Dilemma.* New York: Hill and Wang, 1984.

Mitchell, Henry, and Nicholas C. Lewter. *Soul Theology.* San Francisco: Harper & Row Publishers, 1986.

Moltmann, Jurgen. *Theology of Hope.* New York/San Francisco: Harper & Row Publishers, 1967.

Nouwen, Henri J. M. *The Wounded Healer: Ministry in Contemporary Society,* 2nd ed. New York: Image Doubleday, 1972.

Oden, Thomas C. *Crisis Ministries: Classical Pastoral Care.* New York: Crossroad, 1986.

Parad, Howard J. *Crisis Intervention: Selected Readings*. New York: Family Service Association of America, 1965.

Puryear, Douglas A. *Helping People in Crisis*. San Francisco: Jossey-Bass, 1979.

Raboteau, Albert J. *Slave Religion*. New York: Oxford University Press, 1978.

Rappoport, Lydia. "Crisis Intervention Treatment" in *Theories of Social Casework* by R. W. Roberts. Chicago: University of Chicago Press, 1970.

Schaller, Lyle E. *Strategies for Change*. Nashville: Abingdon Press, 1993.

Schleiermacher, Friedrich. *Christian Caring: Selections from Practical Theology*. Philadelphia: Fortress Press, 2002.

Shelley, Marshall. *Ministering to Problem People in Your Church: What to Do with Well-Intentioned Dragons*. Minneapolis: Bethany House Publishers, 1985.

Shelp, Earl E., and Ronald Sunderland, eds. *A Biblical Basis for Ministry*. Philadelphia: The Westminster Press, 1981.

Shulman, Lawrence. *The Skills of Helping*. Itasca: F. E. Peacock Publishers, 1984.

Spencer, Anita. *Crises and Growth*. New York: Paulist Press, 1989.

Steinke, Peter L. *Healthy Congregations: A Systems Approach*. New York: Rowman & Littlefield, 1996.

Stone, Howard K. *Crisis Counseling*. Philadelphia: Fortress Press, 1974.

Stone, Howard W. *The Caring Church*. San Francisco: Harper & Row Publishers, 1983.

Switzer, David K. *The Minister as Crisis Counselor*. Nashville: Abingdon Press, 1974.

Turabian, Kate L. *A Manual for Writers of Term Papers, Theses, and Dissertations*. Chicago: The University of Chicago Press, 1973.

Vaughn, Joe. *Family Intervention: Hope for Families Struggling with Alcohol and Drugs*. Louisville: Westminster/John Knox, 1989.

Walker, Williston, Richard Norris, David Lotz, and Robert T. Handy. *A History of the Christian Church*. New York: Charles Scribner's Sons, 1985.

Warren, Donald. *Helping Networks*. Indiana: University of Notre Dame, 1981.

Whitney, Curtis L. *Doctoral Dissertation: Developing a Team of Lay Caregivers for Short Term Crisis Care*. Ann Arbor: UMI, 1991.

Wilmore, Gayraud, and James H. Cone. *Black Theology: A Documentary History, 1966–1979*. Maryknoll: Orbis Books, 1979.

Wimberly, Edward P. *Pastoral Counseling & Spiritual Values: A Black Point of View*. Nashville: Abingdon Press, 1982.

_____*A Conceptual Model for Pastoral Care in the Black Church Utilizing Systems and Crisis Theories*. Boston: University Graduate School, Xerox University Microfilms, 1976.

_____*Pastoral Care in the Black Church*. Nashville: Abingdon Press, 1979.

Periodicals

Adelphi University. "School of Social Work. Handbook of Course Readings, Foundation Practice I." Lexington: Ginn Press, 1987–1989.

Browning, Don S. "Mapping the Terrain of Pastoral Theology Toward a Practical Theology of Care." *Pastoral Psychology* 36 (1).

Benner, Patricia. "Caring Practice in the Church." *Laity Exchange*. San Leandro: Vespers Service, September 1987.

Blundall, Joan. "As the Heartland Bleeds, Where Is the Church?" *Laity Exchange*. San Leandro: Vespers Service, July 1987.

Bufford, Rodger K., Buckler, Robert E. "Counseling in the Church: A Proposed Strategy for Ministering to Mental Health Needs in the Church." *Journal of Pastoral Counseling* 6, no. 2 (Summer 1987).

Jones, Lawrence. "Transmitting the Faith." *Journal of Religious Thought* 46, no. 1 (1989).

Lattimore, Vergel, III. "The Positive Contribution of Black Cultural Values to Pastoral Counseling." *The Journal of Pastoral Care* XXXVI, no. 2 (1982).

Lukens, Horace C. Jr. "Lay Counselor Training Revisited: Reflections of a Trainer." *Journal of Pastoral Counseling* 6 (Summer 1987).

Oglesby, William Jr. "Lay Pastoral Care Revisited." *The Journal of Pastoral Care* XXXX, no. 2 (June 1986).

Prater, Jeffrey S. "Training Christian Lay Counselors: Techniques of Prevention and Outreach." *Journal of Pastoral Counseling* 6 (Summer 1987).

Sunderland, Ronald D. Ed. "Lay Pastoral Care." *The Journal of Pastoral Care* XLII, no. 2 (Summer 1988).

Sweeten, Gary. "Lay Helpers and the Caring Community." *Journal of Pastoral Counseling* 6, no. 2 (Summer 1987).

Trulear, Harold Dean. "Reshaping Black Pastoral Theology: The Vision of Bishop Ida B. Robinson." *Journal of Religious Thought* 46, no. 1 (Summer–Fall 1989).

Vos, Nelson. "Your Local Congregation: Is it Salt and Leaven and Light in the World?" *Laity Exchange*. San Leandro: Vespers Service, September 1988.

Wood, Gregg D. "Paying Peter and Paul: Benefits of a Hospital-based Lay Pastoral Visitation Program." *The Journal of Pastoral Care* XL, no. 3 (September 1986).

Bibles/Commentaries

The Interpreters Dictionary of the Bible, Supplementary Volume. Nashville: Abingdon Press, 1962.

The King James Version of the Bible.

Knox, John. *The Interpreter's Bible.* The Gospel According to St. Luke. Nashville: Abingdon, 1952, Vol. 8.

CPSIA information can be obtained
at www.ICGtesting.com
Printed in the USA
BVHW041038080719
552848BV00010B/304/P

9 781973 664406